The Costly Anointing

by Lori Wilke

Destiny Image® Publishers, Inc.
P.O. Box 351
Shippensburg, PA 17257-0351

"We Publish the Prophets"

ISBN 1-56043-051-6

Printed in the U.S.A.
For Worldwide Distribution

Fourth Printing: 1995   Fifth Printing: 1996

This book and all other Destiny Image
and Treasure House books are available
at Christian bookstores and distributors worldwide.

For a U.S. bookstore nearest you,
call **1-800-722-6774**.
For more information on foreign distributors,
call **717-532-3040**.
Or reach us on the Internet: **http://www.reapernet.com**

There is a world-wide hunger to know and understand the anointing of God. Lori Wilke has put together one of the most detailed and in-depth studies that I have read on the subject. She unveils the cost of the anointing, what it is, where it comes from and who will walk in it. I recommend this study of these important principles in your church or personal time, so that together we can fulfill the purpose of God on the earth.

Roberts Liardon

I have known Lori for the past several years. In all my time spent with Lori and her husband, Tom (during their time in my Bible College and in our ministering together), Lori has proven faithful—faithful to God and His anointing, faithful to the call that is upon her life, faithful to whatever she is doing at the time, faithful to those in authority.

The anointing Lori carries (and uses correctly) definitely allows her the right to expound upon it in this book. She is a wonderful servant of God, true to and careful with His anointing.

Norvel Hayes

Contents

FOREWORD

Sound the trumpet! The days of prideful and unholy men preaching cheap grace and misrepresenting the character of Father God are over... Unnoticed by the world, a glorious remnant of Christians is quietly moving into place, taking their ranks in the army of God. Unlike the vast array of those who preceded them throughout the history of the Church, these highly disciplined soldiers have so taken on the mannerisms and countenance of their Chief and Commanding Officer that they are barely distinguishable from Him.

A dream or reality? There is a place of identification with Christ where we take on His character and fragrance—the costly anointing. Called, chosen and faithful servants know the testing and price of the anointing and of fellowship with God. Over and over, they have chosen the more narrow and lonely of two roads. Yet nothing can compare with the priceless treasure they possess.

In *The Costly Anointing*, Lori Wilke beautifully illustrates and characterizes this chosen remnant of the Church as a set apart group taken from the Body of Christ. For those who desire to know God and do His mighty exploits, the precious anointing is available, but it comes at a great cost: everything. These pages shout a battle cry to all God's holy soldiers who not only want their marching orders, but have a revelation that the spiritual battle is intensifying. Only those committed to worship, intercession and fellowship with the Lord will stand.

Dr. Gary L. Greenwald
Eagle's Nest Ministries
Irvine, California

The first time I met Lori Wilke we were both guests on the "Richard Roberts Show." A few weeks later Lori and her husband, Thomas, visited our church in Atlanta. I was impressed with Lori's gifted singing and worship ministry, but even more I sensed in Tom and Lori a dynamic young couple who wanted to serve the Lord with all their hearts.

That spiritual intensity is the essence of Lori's book, *The Costly Anointing*. Serving as somewhat of a spiritual father to Tom and Lori, I am especially grateful to the Lord for the depth and power of this message.

At a time when the anointing of God is being poured out upon the sons and daughters of the Kingdom of God, Lori has sought, experienced and shared extraordinary insights on true anointing. Such a study will lead the reader step by step to greater spiritual discernment and more vibrant Christian service.

If the message of the gospel of the Kingdom is the gravitational word of this generation of the Church—and I am convinced it is—then *The Costly Anointing* becomes a useful manual for Christians who want to bear spiritual fruit that shall remain. Kingdom demonstration is impossible without genuine anointing.

The chorus of one of our favorite songs at Chapel Hill Harvester Church, written by Jimiearl Swilley, says,

"It's the anointing that makes the difference;
Once you have known it, you'll never be the same.
You can't live without it, once it's rested upon you;
It will show you how to walk in Jesus' name."

Indeed, it is the anointing that "makes the difference." For any Christian wanting that difference to minister to others and to glorify the Lord in all they say and do, *The Costly Anointing* turns the key to open your spirit for the anointing oil to flow, flow, flow!

Our King Cometh!

Bishop Earl Paulk, Th.D., D.D.
Chapel Hill Harvester Church
Atlanta, Georgia

Introduction

There is a serious call being sent to the Church in this hour. Most would agree it is a critical time for the Church. Many are at the point of decision, destiny and crossroads. They are hearing a call regarding their part in the final purpose and plan of God. They are sensing an urgency to become everything God has said they should be. If anything is evident right now, it is that God is asking His people to change—no, He is *requiring* that we change.

As we listen to what the Spirit is saying, we hear a call to war and a call to be a demonstration of the Kingdom of God on the earth. We are being summoned by the Spirit to hear the sound of the trumpet of God's prophetic voice. Before God does anything through His Church, He declares it through the mouth of His prophets.

> *Surely the Lord God will do nothing, but he revealeth his secret unto his servants the prophets. The lion hath roared, who will not fear? the Lord God hath spoken, who can but prophesy?*
>
> Amos 3:7-8

The sound of the trumpet is a type of God's prophetic voice proclaiming the Word of the Lord. Paul the apostle said, "For if the trumpet give an uncertain sound, who shall prepare himself to the battle?" We must have both a clear prophetic word and ears to hear it.

In Numbers chapter ten, four things were proclaimed by the trumpet:

1. *The assembling of the camps.* This represents the Body of Christ being drawn together around the presence of the Lord, regardless of group or denomination. The unity of the Spirit we are to pursue is a coming into agreement and submission to the Lordship of Jesus, not a compromise agreement with each other. Jesus' prayer for His Body to "be one" will be answered as we make Him Lord and follow the cloud of His Spirit.

2. *The journeying of the camps.* Each group in the Church is being called to go on with God into new realms in the Spirit. God is calling His people to go where no one has gone before. This requires faith, obedience and a ruthless commitment to leave our comfortable, systematic theologies of serving God.

3. *The preparation for war.* God is gathering His army together to go out to "utterly destroy the inhabitants of the land." It's time to stop fighting one another and to assemble together as one man. We must stop persecuting others in His Body and declare war on the real enemy. This is an hour of warfare and confrontation with the kingdom of darkness, but we must hear the clear and certain sound of the trumpet.

4. *The celebration of the feasts.* The Church has experienced a spiritual fulfillment of the Feast of Passover and the Feast of Pentecost. The trumpet is sounding for the third and final feast, the Feast of Tabernacles, to be fulfilled. Each feast that Israel celebrated in the natural, the Church is to experience in the spirit. It is evident that the Church is about to enter the most intensive spiritual experience it has ever seen. We are about to see the manifestation of the culmination of prayers and prophecies that have been spoken in ages past.

With the fulfillment of the Feast of Tabernacles will come great unity and joy among His people. There will be a great ingathering of souls and the glory of God will be seen upon His people. We shall enter the times of restoration of all things in preparation for His final appearing.

All of this may sound exciting, but it is overwhelming in the power of our own might. We must learn to do all things by His Spirit, under His command and *with the anointing.*

> *And it shall come to pass in that day, that his burden shall be taken away from off thy shoulder, and his yoke from off thy neck, and the yoke shall be destroyed because of the anointing.*

Isaiah 10:27

This anointing, the power of the Holy Spirit, has always been symbolized by oil, especially the "holy anointing oil" of the Old Testament. Each ingredient in this oil has a special significance to our lives. This is a very "costly" oil and represents the process of God's anointing being poured out in our lives. Gethsemane means "oil press," revealing that the way we can be anointed for our divine call is to yield totally to God's will and deny our own.

Whenever our will is "pressed" into doing His will, it will produce a costly oil known as "the anointing."

As the Body of Christ, we are called to walk as He walked and to carry on the work of the Kingdom as the Son has patterned and commanded us to do. Jesus was anointed to preach the gospel to the poor, heal the brokenhearted, preach deliverance to the captives, bring sight to the blind and set at liberty those that were bruised (Luke 4:18-19).

If Jesus, the Son, needed the anointing to minister and to deliver people out of the captivity of sin and of satan, then we need it even more.

We see "how God anointed Jesus of Nazareth with the Holy Ghost and with power: who went about doing good, and healing all that were oppressed of the devil; for God was with him" (Acts 10:38).

It was the anointing of the Holy Spirit that made Jesus effective and successful, not His education, appearance, talents or connections with important people.

God has given the anointing of the Holy Spirit to each believer, that each may be taught, led and empowered for His work. You may be a teacher, a pastor, an evangelist, a prophet or an apostle. You may be a mother, a student, a truck driver or a construction worker. You may be a musician, a songwriter or an artist. It makes no difference. God's plan for His people doesn't change because of the methods or the vessels. His desire is to use every gift, every calling and every available tool for one purpose and one end: to minister His love to a lost and dying humanity.

> *But the anointing which ye have received of him abideth in you, and ye need not that any man teach you: but as the same anointing teacheth you of all things, and is truth, and is no lie, and even as it hath taught you, ye shall abide in him.*
>
> First John 2:27

No matter what He calls us to do on this earth, it will bear no fruit unless we abide in Him. We must lay down the armor of the flesh and put on the complete and powerful armor of God.

Now is the time for this special army of people to arise in the image and likeness of the Son of God. This will be a generation that will do all that God puts in their heart to do. It will be a people that will pay any price and do whatever it takes to walk *in the costly anointing.*

Pastor Thomas Wilke
Milwaukee, Wisconsin

Then took Mary a pound of ointment of spikenard, very costly, and anointed the feet of Jesus, and wiped his feet with her hair: and the house was filled with the odour of the ointment.

John 12:3

Part I

The Anointing

...the yoke shall be destroyed because of the anointing.

Isaiah 10:27

Chapter 1

Preparing for a
New Anointing

God is requiring change—change in our lifestyles, change in our attitudes, change in our relationships and change in our ministries. This change, and it's a radical one, will affect everyone in the Body of Christ to some degree. Some will like it, some will hate it, some will submit to it and some will rebel against it. No matter who you are, you cannot be neutral. God is confronting you and calling you.

God is asking us to prepare our hearts for changes that will be coming to pass both in the Church and in the world. As we do this there will come a refining and a spiritual cleansing in our lives. This will enable us to behold God, to be changed from glory to glory and to be entrusted with His power and ability.

And he shall sit as a refiner and purifier of silver: and he shall purify the sons of Levi, and purge them as gold and silver, that they may offer unto the Lord an offering in righteousness.... For I am the Lord, I change not; therefore ye sons of Jacob are not consumed.

Malachi 3:3,6

The Need for a New Anointing

People who have been in the Church for a time seem to grow stiff, starchy and very legalistic. Yet God wants us to grow in the knowledge of His grace, not the works of the law. Many of us have need of an oil change, a fresh filling of the Holy Spirit. Just as oil can dry up and evaporate, so can the anointing wane and diminish if it is not properly supplied. Fresh fellowship with the Holy Spirit will produce fresh oil.

A major problem today is that we have so many things to do. We have people to see, places to go, things to do. Who did we see? Where did we go? What did we do? Umm... Well, it seemed important at the time. Ask yourself this question: How does what you do affect your relationship with God? Is it fulfilling your calling, your vision, your destiny in God? He understands schedules and needs, but He is asking us to get our priorities straight!

When Jesus walked on the earth He faced every temptation and experience we do. Before He left, He said, "I will not leave you comfortless." So He sent us the Comforter, the one with the anointing. He is our Companion, Helper, Advocate, Friend, Strength and Counselor.

We need to talk directly to Him, not just about Him. He wants us to fellowship with Him and share every part of our lives with Him as we would a trusted friend. We can invite Him to counsel us, instruct us and help us with every detail of our lives. We can watch His faithfulness, experience His love and trust His wisdom as He works in our lives. King David prayed:

4

> *Create in me a clean heart, O God; and renew a right spirit within me. Cast me not away from thy presence; and take not thy holy spirit from me. Restore unto me the joy of my salvation; and uphold me with thy free spirit. Then will I teach transgressors thy ways; and sinners shall be converted unto thee.*
>
> Psalm 51:10-13

A fresh anointing oil from Heaven will restore your joy. If you have lost your peace, get a fresh touch of Holy Spirit oil. The anointing oil of Heaven will heal your spirit, soul and body. It will work miracles in your home, in your job and in your church.

The Softening of the Spirit

> *And he spake also a parable unto them; No man putteth a piece of a new garment upon an old; if otherwise, then both the new maketh a rent, and the piece that was taken out of the new agreeth not with the old. And no man putteth new wine into old bottles; else the new wine will burst the bottles, and be spilled, and the bottles shall perish. But new wine must be put into new bottles; and both are preserved. No man also having drunk old wine straightway desireth new: for he saith, The old is better.*
>
> Luke 5:36-39

In Bible times skins were used as containers for liquids. Over a period of time the skins dried out and became hard and brittle. When that happened they were dipped in water and then rubbed with oil to soften and restore them so that they could be used again. If they were not processed in this way, they became useless because of their hardness and lack of flexibility.

Jesus gave this example as a pattern of what He wants to do in His Church. Our dried and hardened hearts must be changed into soft and pliable vessels, prepared to yield to His will and contain His new wine. How each heart experiences this change may vary, but the principle is the same. If we're not flexible, we must be softened by the Spirit or we will break trying to receive the new wine.

New wine represents a new move of God's Spirit or a fresh outpouring of the anointing for a specific purpose in the plan of God. We must know how to prepare ourselves and what we must do to contain the new anointing when it comes, for it shall surely come.

The old crusty wineskins were first dipped in water to restore moisture. This is symbolic of our hearts being moistened by "the washing of water by the word." Without this cleansing we build up walls of resistance and unbelief which keep us from receiving the flow of the Spirit's power. The wineskins were then rubbed with fresh oil to bring added flexibility and endurance. This fresh oil, which is representative of a new anointing in our lives, is what gives us the ability to move on with God and walk in the new wine of His Spirit.

The word "anointing" actually means "to rub" and can be interpreted as meaning "to smear with oil." The dried and crusty Church of this day needs a new wineskin. There are many changes that need to be made in our hearts and lives. As we prepare to receive that change from God, we can rely on His promise: It is "not by might, nor by power, but by my spirit, saith the Lord of hosts."

Davidic Pattern for the Anointing

David was one of the most anointed people mentioned in Scripture. He was a prophet (Acts 2:29-30), he was a king (II Sam. 2:1-7), and he was a psalmist. Second Samuel 23:1 says, "Now these be the last words of David. David the son of Jesse said, and

6

the man who was raised up on high, the anointed of the God of Jacob, and the sweet psalmist of Israel..." David received three distinct anointings.

First, David was anointed "in the midst of his brethren." First Samuel 16:13 says, "Then Samuel took the horn of oil, and anointed him in the midst of his brethren: and the spirit of the Lord came upon David from that day forward." Second, David was anointed as King over the house of Judah. We read in Second Samuel 2:4, "And the men of Judah came, and there they anointed David king over the house of Judah..." Third, David was anointed as King over all Israel. "So all the elders of Israel came to the king to Hebron; and king David made a league with them in Hebron before the Lord: and they anointed David king over Israel" (II Sam. 5:3). In Psalm 92, David listed seven things that the anointing will do for us:

But my horn shalt thou exalt like the horn of an unicorn: I shall be anointed with fresh oil. Mine eye also shall see my desire on mine enemies, and mine ears shall hear my desire of the wicked that rise up against me. The righteous shall flourish like the palm tree: he shall grow like a cedar in Lebanon. Those that be planted in the house of the Lord shall flourish in the courts of our God. They shall still bring forth fruit in old age; they shall be fat and flourishing; to shew that the Lord is upright: he is my rock, and there is no unrighteousness in him.

Psalm 92:10-15

1. "Mine eye...shall see." The anointing will give us a new vision. We need God's vision to establish goals and fulfill our destiny in the Kingdom. Those who live without a vision, without purpose, live in hopelessness and depression. Cases of suicide are an example of this. That is why the Scriptures say, "Where there is no vision, the people perish" (Prov.

7

29:18). God has a vision for everyone. The anointing will help us to see that vision and walk in it. Habakkuk 2:2 says, "Write the vision, and make it plain upon tables, that he may run that readeth it." Many never reach their potential because they can't see God's dream for their life. If a person doesn't press in and wait upon the Lord, he will give up too soon. Verse 3 says, "For the vision is yet for an appointed time, but at the end it shall speak, and not lie: though it tarry, wait for it; because it will surely come, it will not tarry." No price is too high to pay for God's dream for your life. God will spare no expense to give His vision to those who seek Him. "Anoint thine eyes with eye-salve, that thou mayest see" (Rev. 3:18).

2. "Mine ears shall hear." The anointing will open your ears so you can hear God's voice. As sons and daughters of God we need to be led by the Spirit. Many love to read and study the Bible, but have never heard God's personal, intimate voice. The anointing will give you spiritual ears so that you can hear the living Word of God, which is clear, definite and specific. God's still, small voice offers solutions to problems and recognizable answers to hidden or unconfessed sin. In contrast, the enemy will be indefinite, vague and imaginary in his accusing and condemning language. Usually no real solutions are offered and that which he gives is irrational and unscriptural, resulting in confusion and unbelief. When we purpose in our heart to unconditionally obey the voice of God, then He is faithful to direct us.

3. "The righteous shall flourish like the palm tree." A palm tree has deep roots that search out the water in desert places. If we will take the time to develop a deep relationship with the Holy Spirit, it will be like "a well of water springing up into everlasting life" (John 4:14). The anointing will aid you in finding watering places in deserts and during dry seasons.

8

This brings confidence that you can flourish and bear fruit no matter where you are planted. Let your roots grow deep in the soil of God's love. Be confident in this: No pit is so deep that God's love is not deeper still. "Therefore with joy shall you draw water out of the wells of salvation" (Is. 12:3).

4. "He shall grow like a cedar in Lebanon." Cedars have a very long life. There are principles in the Kingdom that, if observed, will bring length of days, riches and honor. The Scriptures are filled with these principles: "Let your heart keep His commandments," "find wisdom," "get understanding," "receive instruction," "develop humility," "gain the fear of the Lord" and "find the knowledge of the Holy One" (Prov. 3:1,2,13-16; 4:13; 22:4; 9:10-11).

5. "Those that be planted in the house of the Lord shall flourish in the courts of our God." It is God's desire that we should bring forth much fruit and that our fruit should remain. This requires dedication and patience to commit to the task we are given and the place to which we are called. This means we must make a covenant (a promise to do or die) with God and those who He has called us to work with. The reason many never bear fruit is simply that they run from commitment and fear the rejection of failure. They never plant themselves with people or tend the garden of godly relationships. How many pastors have heard someone say, "God told me to come here and do this or that," yet after a few months or even weeks that one is nowhere to be found? God uses those He can find, those who are planted in His house.

The blessings of God come when you are planted firmly in His habitation. This involves commitment to God, His Church, His people and His presence. Whenever you give yourself, seeding your prayers, your time and your finances into the storehouse of God, you will liberally receive His many fringe benefits. Don't be shy! "They went out from us, but they were not of us; for if they had been of us, they would no doubt have continued with us: but they went out, that they might be made manifest that they were not all of us. But ye have an unction [anointing] from the Holy One, and ye know all things" (I John 2:19-20). The anointing will cause us to flourish three ways: in giving us commitment to be where God wants us to be, in equipping us to do what God has called us to do, and in revealing the truth about our situation so we won't believe a lie.

6. "They shall still bring forth fruit in old age." This is the heritage of the servants of the Lord. Many of God's servants received their promise late in life. Take Abraham and Sarah for an example. He was one hundred years old and she was well advanced in years when they conceived and gave birth to Isaac. Elizabeth conceived John the mighty prophet after it was physically impossible to do so. Caleb received the land of Hebron, his promised inheritance, when he was eighty-five, after waiting forty-five years in the wilderness. Each of these servants wholly followed the Lord and the anointing brought forth the promise at the appointed time. As God prospers us through the anointing we will live longer and be more fruitful.

7. "To shew that the Lord is upright: he is my rock, and there is no unrighteousness in him." The anointing will bring forth purity in your life and will reveal that purity to the world. This is probably the most beautiful of the seven thoughts. The Lord is upright, pure and holy, making those who associate with Him upright, pure and holy. The world will see this truth as we are changed from glory to glory by the Spirit of the Lord. The key is to reject the dry and crusty thoughts that would make our wineskin useless and to submit

moment by moment to the gentle massage of His Word and His Spirit.

Faith for the Anointing

In order to receive the anointing of the Holy Spirit we must develop our faith in it and allow God to deal with those areas in us that would hinder its flow. The more we open ourselves to receive His instruction, the more He can lead us in the way we should go. Always remember, God's not looking for ability, but *availability*. He doesn't need perfect vessels, He needs *willing* vessels. Faith in God's grace and ability will help keep the anointing from diminishing. Faith is essential. Faith has action and faith has a voice! When faith hears, it speaks. When faith sees, it takes immediate action. It doesn't wonder or complain about its circumstances; it believes in the grace of God.

There are many things that will cause the anointing oil to leak out of our vessel. One of them is *unbelief.* Unbelief is not the same thing as doubt. The difference is that doubt doesn't believe what God has said because it doesn't know what He has said. On the other hand, unbelief knows what God has said but refuses to believe. Unbelief will keep us from entering our inheritance just as it did the children of Israel.

> *Take heed, brethren, lest there be in any of you an evil heart of unbelief, in departing from the living God.... So we see that they could not enter in [into the promised land] because of unbelief.*
>
> Hebrews 3:12,19

A second hindrance to the anointing is *stubbornness* and *rebellion.* To refuse God's revealed will in your life or to openly reject His commands is simply pride and arrogance. Even serving God in our own way is still rebellion. We can't have our own version of

11

serving God. We can't obey His Word the way we feel comfortable or the way we see it to be. Our flesh and the devil will *never* be comfortable doing God's will.

> *And Samuel said, Hath the Lord as great delight in burnt offerings and sacrifices, as in obeying the voice of the Lord? Behold, to obey is better than sacrifice, and to hearken than the fat of rams. For rebellion is as the sin of witchcraft, and stubbornness is as iniquity and idolatry. Because thou hast rejected the word of the Lord, he hath also rejected thee from being king.*
>
> First Samuel 15:22-23

Saul, who was anointed to be king over Israel, was told by the Lord through the prophet Samuel to "smite Amalek, and utterly destroy all that they have, and spare them not." But Saul had his own version of what God had told him. Because he "feared the people and obeyed their voice," he created his own interpretation of God's word.

> *And Samuel said, When thou wast little in thine own sight, wast thou not made the head of the tribes of Israel, and the Lord anointed thee king over Israel?*
>
> First Samuel 15:17

Saul's anointing was removed because he assumed he knew the mind of the Lord rather than diligently inquiring of Him. He did what seemed best because he feared being rejected by the people. The root cause of most rebellion is the fear of rejection. This fear can be eliminated by receiving significance, security and acceptance from God rather than people. In order to receive this, one must come to Him believing in His love and that He is a rewarder of those who diligently continue to seek Him (Heb. 11:6).

Thirdly, when we yield to *sinful pleasures,* a wall goes up between us and God. Our heart is not made to serve two masters. Jesus said, "No man can serve two masters: for either he will hate the one, and love the other; or else he will hold to the one, and despise the other" (Matt. 6:24). We are daily confronted with decisions that influence our relationship with God. If our heart condemns us we can't have confidence before Him. Any kind of persistent sin will slowly rob us of the anointing. When we stay in God's presence, His fire will consume the chaff of fleshly desires and bring forth the works of God which are like gold, silver and precious stones.

Some people want the blessing of the Lord, but they love flirting with the world more than they love Him. They want their flesh to be gratified before they will serve Him. If we desire to reap from the Spirit we must sow to the Spirit. Whatever we sow ourselves into is what we will reap. We must develop a revelation of His love and love Him with the intensity with which He loves us. That relationship of love will carry us through every valley of life.

A fourth area hindering the anointing is a *broken heart.* So many members of the Body of Christ have been hurt, mistreated and taken advantage of. They have been hurt so deeply somewhere in the past that they feel they can never risk loving again. This hinders their developing an intimate relationship with God. If you are willing to give Jesus the chance, He knows how to totally heal your broken heart. That's what He's anointed to do. God has made special provision for the brokenhearted. He knows that broken people are afraid or ashamed to reach out to Him, so He draws very near to them.

> *The Lord is nigh unto them that are of a broken heart; and saveth such as be of a contrite spirit.*
>
> Psalm 34:18

In order to walk in the high calling of God for our lives, we must keep our oil thick, rich and fresh. If the oil in your car's engine gets old and thin, you must replace it. You wouldn't risk ruining an expensive engine. Don't risk losing your soul or the souls of others. Get a new filling. Old oil stinks, but fresh oil has a lovely smell. Some Christians stink. They are offensive to the people around them. They may think they smell like Oscar de la Renta's perfume, but they stink if they are operating on old oil. The oil you received two years ago won't serve the purpose. The oil of a month or a day ago won't serve the purpose. You need fresh oil from Heaven today!

If you start feeling cranky with people around you, you need fresh oil. People enjoyed being around Jesus. Do they enjoy being around you? If you need fresh oil, yield to Him right now. Let Him begin to massage you with that oil. Let Him work the hardness out of your soul. Let Him soften your heart and let the miracle of a new anointing begin today!

Chapter 2

The Anointing Oil and the Sacred Perfume

The ingredients used to make the anointing oil in Old Testament times hold great significance for us today. These elements picture the characteristics of God in the anointing. Once these traits are developed in our lives, the anointing will flow unhindered and in great fulness. Many believers have limited the anointing to that portion pertaining to the gifts, not realizing the same anointing teaches them concerning the nature of God. This involves a growth process in which we behold the Lord as in a dark glass or an unclear mirror, maturing us from glory to glory. The depth of the anointing is directly related to an individual's submission to the Spirit in the personal development of *both* the gifts and the fruits. Some people have wonderful gifts, but because the fruit of the Spirit has not been developed in them they are not effective.

The Old Testament priests wore a beautiful garment on which were bells and pomegranates. The bells represent the gifts of God, the endowments of the Holy Spirit to us. The pomegranates represent the fruit of God or His character within us. The two must go hand and hand in order for God to release through us the beauty of His anointing in the fulness that He desires. We need a balance of the reality of God.

The fruit of the Spirit not only accompanies the gifts of the Spirit, but helps to develop the gifts. Without the nature of God, the gifts themselves will short-circuit and deplete. The fruit serves to enhance the gifts and to bring them forth with grace and beauty. The anointing, therefore, is two-fold, encompassing both the gifts and the fruits of the Spirit. Both are imparted to the believer as a divine unction from God.

> *But the anointing which ye have received of him abideth in you, and ye need not that any man teach you: but as the same anointing teacheth you of all things, and is truth, and is no lie, and even as it hath taught you, ye shall abide in him.*

> First John 2:27

The growth process in the anointing requires us to behold the character and beauty of the Lord as in a mirror, and to be changed into the same image. This process often involves a "breaking before a making." The Church will need to reckon itself dead to sin and alive unto God concerning many specific habit structures defiling the human character. This requires humility and much God-given grace. This mandate looms before our hearts and minds: Follow on to know the Lord.

Through the ages God has often used types and shadows to speak to His people. What God has concealed in the Old Testament as similitudes has been revealed in the New Testament in the Person of Christ. For example, in the Old Testament the anointing always took on a three-fold nature. First, there were the anointers, such as Samuel and Elisha. Second, there were the ones being anointed, such as Aaron and David. Third was the anointing, seen in the holy anointing oil. The New Testament also reveals to us these three-fold realities of the anointing in the Godhead. First, the Father is the Anointer. "God anointed Jesus of Nazareth with the Holy Ghost and with power: who went about doing good, and healing all that were oppressed of the devil; for God was with him" (Acts 10:38). Second, the Son is the Anointed. "He first findeth his own brother Simon, and saith unto him, We have found the Messiah, which is, being interpreted, the anointed one" (John 1:41, paraphrased). Third, the Holy Spirit is the Anointing (I John 2:20,27). These examples of the triunity of the Godhead in its nature and function help us see the administration of the anointing.

Since the Lord Jesus is the Christ, the anointed, the believers which constitute His body received the same anointing. Christ, being the Head, reigns over the members of His Body (I Cor. 12:12,27). Christians are anointed ones, members of Christ. The Holy Spirit is that precious anointing oil that abides within us.

Outlined for us in the composition of the anointing oil itself are natural examples with great spiritual imagery, significance and instruction.

In the Book of Exodus, under the instructions given by the Lord to Moses concerning the Tabernacle of Moses, we have specific directions pertaining to this holy oil.

> *Take thou also unto thee principal spices, of pure myrrh five hundred shekels, and of sweet cinnamon half so much, even two hundred and fifty shekels, and of sweet calamus two hundred and fifty shekels, and of cassia five hundred shekels, after the shekel of the sanctuary, and of oil olive an hin: and thou shalt make it an oil of holy ointment, an ointment compound after the art of the apothecary: it shall*

> *be an holy anointing oil. And thou shalt anoint the taber-*
> *nacle of the congregation therewith, and the ark of the*
> *testimony...*

Exodus 30:23-26

Pure Myrrh

Myrrh is a resin (gum) that oozed from a tiny shrub. Although it was very bitter to the taste, it produced a fragrance so pleasing that it had great value in biblical times. The word *myrrh* literally means "bitter." It was one of the three gifts that the wise men brought to Jesus after His birth. Each of these gifts was a type of the three offices in which Jesus walked, namely, prophet, priest and king. Myrrh speaks of the office of the prophet, and therefore is most bitter. Jesus was a Man of sorrow, both in His life and in His death. His true joy came from obedient service to His Father. To the believer, myrrh symbolizes a life of true discipleship to the Lord.

> *So likewise, whosoever he be of you that forsaketh not all*
> *that he hath, he cannot be my disciple.*

Luke 14:33

In order for Jesus to become the perfect Sacrifice, He learned obedience "by the things which he suffered" (Heb. 5:8). In the same way, so that the anointing may be developed in us and flow out of us, we must deal with some bitter facts. A disciple is a follower, a student of Christ. He has purposed in his heart that, at any cost, he will follow the steps of his Master. Jesus gave us the example. He, the greatest of all, took a towel and a basin and washed the feet of His disciples. The flavor of discipleship and service may taste a bit bitter, but, as the servant is no greater than the master, we as followers of Christ lay aside our selfish desires to follow the Lord. If Jesus washed feet, we are called to learn the same obedience as Christ, the suffering Servant. Conquer your pride and put self aside! Put flesh in its place to become the servant of grace.

18

Serving others requires that we take the lowest place among the brethren of Christ. In order to be great in the Lord's eyes, the believer's heart must be set on such things as loving those who have nothing to give in return, serving others behind the scenes where no one can applaud, and being content to take a supporting role to help a leader secure a spiritual trophy. Service involves all this and more. Are you ready for greatness? Our joy is found in forsaking all to follow the call of God.

> *And whosoever doth not bear his cross, and come after me, cannot be my disciple.*
>
> Luke 14:27

The cross represents our responsibilities as His servants. As His disciples we cannot learn His ways if our ways are more important to us. The anointing oil of the Spirit abides and is developed in those who have laid down their lives for Him.

Sweet Cinnamon

Cinnamon comes from the bark of a tree and has a certain fragrant sweetness. The root meaning of the word *cinnamon* is "to erect" or "to stand upright." Cinnamon here represents integrity and walking in truth. The flower of the cinnamon tree smells offensive, but the bark is sweet. This represents God's people who are living among a corrupt and perverted society with a challenge to divinely influence it.

> *Do all things without murmurings and disputings: that ye may be blameless and harmless, the sons of God, without rebuke, in the midst of a crooked and perverse nation, among whom ye shine as lights in the world; holding forth the word of life; that I may rejoice in the day of Christ, that I have not run in vain, neither laboured in vain.*
>
> Philippians 2:14-16

19

Although everything around us may stink, we can maintain purity and sweetness. We can shine as lights in this dark world. Jesus was the Light of the world, but notice whence His anointing came: He was "anointed with the oil of gladness above [His] fellows" because He "loved righteousness," and "hated iniquity" (Heb. 1:9). The anointing will rise to the occasion when the need is the greatest. As long as you are in a place of isolation, away from hurting, needing people, the anointing remains untapped. Take a step into Isaiah 61 and find out what makes the anointing come alive. Whenever you reach out to the brokenhearted, the captive, the bruised, the mourning, the desolate, the outcast, you'll also find Jesus and His fragrant anointing. The effects of sin are unpleasant, but the sweet anointing of God covers a multitude of sin. We are set apart as believers; although we are physically in the world, we are not of it.

Those stinky flowers of the cinnamon tree represent the corrupt influences surrounding the Church. Will you as a member of God's Body respond like the rest of the world, or will you set yourself apart to seek the Lord? Will you allow the anointing to aid you in resisting vile influences in order to produce something pleasant? The choice is yours. You can walk in integrity and truth before God, or you can choose the deceit of the enemy. If you make the choice to allow the Word of God to be that which flows from your heart and mouth, the anointing will help you "to will and to do God's good pleasure." Remember that Jesus was anointed with great joy and gladness because He loved righteousness and hated iniquity.

Sweet Calamus

Calamus was a tall reed that grew in the hostile environment of miry clay. The word literally means "a branch" or "a reed." Calamus speaks to us of a living, abiding relationship with Jesus,

20

as the vine is to the branches. The sweet calamus is a rod of strength, a channel, a branch through which the oil can flow. Like the calamus, we are living in a hostile environment that makes it difficult to produce life. Unless we abide in the Vine, maintaining an abiding relationship with Jesus, we will not survive. If we do maintain that relationship, nothing in our environment can keep us from bearing fruit. When an intimate relationship with Jesus is ever increasing, our lives remain fruitful. We can be placed in the worst situations of existence and still sing. "God has set His love upon us, therefore He will deliver us" (Ps. 91:14, paraphrased).

Psalm 137 was written during the captivity of the children of Israel in Babylon.

> *By the rivers of Babylon, there we sat down, yea, we wept, when we remembered Zion. We hanged our harps upon the willows in the midst thereof. For there they that carried us away captive required of us a song; and they that wasted us required of us mirth, saying, Sing us one of the songs of Zion. How shall we sing the Lord's song in a strange land?*
> Psalm 137:1-4

The Body of Christ is held captive in a strange land, but a deep relationship with Jesus will set us free. The devil, the world and the sinful flesh are constantly warring against us. The time has come for God's warriors to arise and conquer the Babylonian system. In the midst of our personal miry clay, our Babylon, satan's condemning voice may be bellowing, "Come on, let me hear you sing now, big mouth! You, who were able to praise God with such fervor when life was easy, let me hear you sing now that I've got you in the pit!"

That is when the grace of God becomes our sufficiency in battle, and in the face of satan and every cohort we echo one of the songs of Zion:

21

Amazing grace! How sweet the sound,
That saved a wretch like me!
I once was lost, but now am found,
Was blind, but now I see.

The branch of the Lord comes bursting forth as the revelation of Jesus' love is illuminated in our heart.

The time we spend seeking the Lord is priceless. God will give us a Kingdom warrior spirit to help us grow in the hard places of life. The fire—the anointing of God—will enable us to shout for joy, even when we don't feel like it. This brings us the victory, for Jesus inhabits our praises. The enemy is confused, for what was intended to wipe us out has made us joyful. Don't be a Kingdom wimp; be a Kingdom warrior!

Cassia

Cassia, like cinnamon, is found in the bark of a shrub. It grows in high altitudes and possesses a little purple flower. Biblically the root of the word means "bowing down" or "shriveled," as in bowing before the Lord in reverent worship. Cassia speaks to us of worshiping the Lord in spirit and truth. If you are dry and weary, know that the anointing of God will come to you as you worship and adore Him. Worship is one of the most important elements of the Christian life. We must come "into His gates with thanksgiving and into His courts with praise" (Ps. 100:4). These times of deep adoration will edify our spirit and keep our mind on Jesus, resulting in perfect peace. Worship softens the heart, enabling us to hear God's voice and walk in step with Him.

The same root word is used when Abraham's servant "bowed down" his head to worship God because he had found the desired wife for Isaac.

And the man bowed down his head, and worshipped the Lord.

Genesis 24:26

And I bowed down my head, and worshipped the Lord, and blessed the Lord God of my master Abraham, which had led me in the right way to take my master's brother's daughter unto his son.

Genesis 24:48

It is also used when David humbled himself in reverence before Saul.

David also arose afterward, and went out of the cave, and cried after Saul, saying, My lord the king. And when Saul looked behind him, David stooped with his face to the earth, and bowed himself.

First Samuel 24:8

It is interesting to note that the first use of the word for worship in the Bible concerns the offering of Isaac on the altar of Moriah. True worship leads to a total surrender to the Lordship of Jesus. Jesus talks about worship as not simply an act, but a state of being. In John chapter four He taught us that it is not how we worship, but where we are spiritually when we worship that matters. Religion always dictates the way we can or cannot worship God. Jesus said that we must worship God in spirit and that the way or method of worship should not be the focus. We must become those who worship in spirit and truth, or all we will have is a miserable performance. Just like the cassia, we seek to bow before the Lord, ministering to Christ that men may see a demonstration of pure love and seek to follow.

The word *cassia* may be rendered "shrivel up" or "stoop." This implies our humbling ourselves in total surrender to God, giving

23

Him all glory, honor and thanksgiving. The true anointing flows out of a heart yielded to the will of the Father. Our submission to the will of God in humility allows Him to lift us to a position of royalty in due time. The cassia grew in high altitudes, symbolizing the exaltation of God after seasons of bowing before Him. The flower on the shrub was purple, representing royalty, the reward of the Lord. "By humility and the fear of the Lord are riches, and honour, and life" (Prov. 22:4). By recognizing the preeminence of God, we are submitting to His Lordship in every aspect of our daily lives.

Thy kingdom come. Thy will be done, Lord! Let your anointing flow through such willing vessels.

Olive Oil

The olive oil was the ingredient that bound all the spices together. This blending together of sweet and bitter speaks of the unity involved in the holy anointing of the Lord upon His ministers. Psalm 133 says,

> *Behold, how good and how pleasant it is for brethren to dwell together in unity! It is like the precious ointment upon the head, that ran down upon the beard, even Aaron's beard: that went down to the skirts of his garments; as the dew of Hermon, and as the dew that descended upon the mountains of Zion: for there the Lord commanded the blessing, even life for evermore.*

Those who make it their aim to bring the Body of Christ together as one will find the anointing abiding and growing in their lives and ministries. Those who, because of insecurity, need to build their own kingdoms and criticize other believers will find the anointing of the Lord beginning to lift from them. The Lord has given His ministries a mandate in Ephesians 4:11-13 which is still applicable today. The gift-ministries we read of there have not yet ceased to be necessary because the call to "come in the unity of the faith" and grow to "the measure of the stature of the fulness of Christ" has not yet been reached by the Church.

The anointing oil upon God's ministers is to perfect the saints and draw them together in the unity of the faith. Jesus' High-Priestly prayer in the garden of Gethsemane was a plea for His disciples and for those who should believe on Him through their word (that means us) to become one even as the Father and Son are one. *Gethsemane* means "oil press," and it was through the costly sufferings of Christ that the holy anointing oil of the Spirit was provided for the Church as one body—that it should become one body.

God told Moses that this anointing oil was so sacred that it must be protected. The same is true today. It is not to be indiscriminately used. "Upon man's flesh shall it not be poured" (Ex. 30:32). God does not anoint the flesh or the feelings of the flesh. We must strip ourselves of the carnality of fleshly desire, just as the priests were required to be cleansed and washed before entering God's presence.

No one may copy the formula of this oil. "Neither shall ye make any other like it" (Ex. 30:32). Imitations of the anointing oil will be judged. The last days will reveal false Christs, false anointed ones upon whom will rest a false anointing. It is easy to pretend to be spiritual or to act like a good Christian, but God who knows the heart will one day say, "Depart from Me, I never knew you."

Leviticus 10:1-2 recounts the judgment against "strange fire."

And Nadab and Abihu, the sons of Aaron, took either of them his censer, and put fire therein, and put incense thereon, and offered strange fire before the Lord, which he

25

> *commanded them not. And there went out fire from the*
> *Lord, and devoured them, and they died before the Lord.*

God is reminding the sons of the High Priests today that playing with the anointing can be like playing with fire—consuming!

Using the anointing for things other than God's purposes is forbidden. "It is holy, and it shall be holy unto you" (Ex. 30:32). The Holy Spirit uses us. We can never use Him. If the anointing becomes commonplace to us or is taken for granted, it will disappear. It must be reverenced and appreciated like a precious gift. "Whosoever compoundeth any like it, or whosoever putteth any of it upon a stranger, shall even be cut off from his people" (Ex. 30:33). We are not to substitute or compromise the anointing for those outside the Church. Many are trying to use the name "Christian" on their activities to try to be acceptable to both God and the world at the same time. Those in this kind of disobedience will never taste of God's holy anointing.

Disregarding God's commands when flowing in the anointing will result in being cut off from your part of the Body (your ministry). The holy oil will not be used except in submission to God's order and design. The anointing is holy and precious. It is costly.

So we see that there were five ingredients blended together to constitute the holy anointing oil. The number five is significant, for it represents the grace of God in the atonement. It is only because of God's abundant grace that the anointing oil is provided. We will look at this grace further in a later chapter.

The Sacred Perfume

At the same time Moses received instructions concerning the holy anointing oil, God told him to make a special sacred perfume that would be placed in the Tabernacle:

26

And the Lord said unto Moses, Take unto thee sweet spices, stacte, and onycha, and galbanum; these sweet spices with pure frankincense: of each shall there be a like weight: and thou shalt make it a perfume, a confection after the art of the apothecary, tempered together, pure and holy: and thou shalt beat some of it very small, and put of it before the testimony in the tabernacle of the congregation, where I will meet with thee: it shall be unto you most holy.

Exodus 30:34-36

Jesus became a pleasing fragrance to God in our behalf and has called us to be a pleasing fragrance to Him.

Be ye therefore followers of God, as dear children; and walk in love, as Christ also hath loved us, and hath given himself for us an offering and a sacrifice to God for a sweet-smelling savour.

Ephesians 5:1-2

Now thanks be unto God, which always causeth us to triumph in Christ, and maketh manifest the savour of his knowledge by us in every place. For we are unto God a sweet savour of Christ, in them that are saved, and in them that perish: To the one we are the savour of death unto death; and to the other the savour of life unto life.

Second Corinthians 2:14-16a

To some we are a fragrance of death. When we walk in the anointing, in the power of God and the fruit of the Spirit, we provoke people, and they can't handle that. Our very presence brings conviction. To the ones hungry for God we have the opposite effect. They want to get close to us. They want to stand beside us. We bring life and joy to their lives, as we do to God. We are "a sweet-smelling savour."

Just as each part of the holy oil is symbolic and speaks to us, so the different parts of the sacred perfume, or incense, speak of how our lives are to be a fragrant aroma to God.

Stacte

The first ingredient in God's perfume was stacte. *Stacte* means "to fall," and "to drop," and denotes a freedom. A beautiful aspect of the anointing is the fact that the gifts and callings of God will flow very naturally and very freely. It may seem like the most natural thing we could do. For the anointing already abides in us as a gift—a calling or an ability. Though the gift is there in its raw form, the Holy Spirit will cultivate and refine this when it is yielded to the Lord. Those who have tried to lean upon the gift in its original form and have not dedicated it to the Lord have found the original endowment of His anointing to be shallow and powerless. When an ability is yielded to God and His glory, it becomes a sharp, powerful and active tool in His hand. "Freely you have received, freely give" (Matt. 10:8).

Onycha

The second ingredient in the perfume was *onycha,* which means "to roar" or "to groan." This substance was extracted from a shellfish found deep in the Red Sea and derived its fragrance from the things upon which the shellfish fed. Jesus said, "Take heed what you hear." The way we feed our spirit is through what we hear. Romans 10:17 says, "So then faith cometh by hearing, and hearing by the word of God." When the life of God is poured into us, the anointing will flow like rivers of living water out from us.

...Out of his belly shall flow rivers of living water.
John 7:38b

The principle of onycha is that the anointing will roar out of the depth of our heart. The revealed Word of God does not come

28

by education, but by revelation. God's Spirit calls to the deep of our spirit. (See Psalm 42:7.)

In order for something to flow out of us, something must first be put in. If we want to give out God's Word, we first need a revelation. Jesus said, "Upon this rock I will build my church" (Matt. 16:18). What rock is this? The rock of revelation. You may have a wonderful gift in your life, but if you don't get a revelation of the Word of God concerning your gift, you will never see it developed to its fulness.

Onycha was very rare and therefore very costly. It is a reminder to us that we must press in to the depths of God's Spirit and pay the price to obtain this special fragrance.

Galbanum

The third ingredient was *galbanum,* which means "fatty" or "rich." It was the sap from a broken shrub. If you observe the lives of those who carry a rich, heavy anointing, you will find that they have been broken and tempered by the Holy Spirit.

> *The sacrifices of God are a broken spirit: a broken and a contrite heart, O God, thou wilt not despise.*
>
> Psalm 51:17

The anointing is designed to teach us all things. Some people seem to learn more quickly and more easily than others. Ideally, we are to "receive with meekness the ingrafted word, which is able to save your souls." With a spirit of humility, we can ask God to take away our traditional, preconceived ideas of God's Word and exchange them for a divinely inspired Spirit to spirit word. This growth process is easy, for we have chosen to fall upon the Rock (Jesus) and to be broken and changed. The rich galbanum then proceeds out of our actions, words and thoughts, bringing a whole new perspective on life. Like a Father, the Lord gently leads us through His disciplines to receive that which makes us "fat": the milk, the bread and the meat of the Word.

Unfortunately, there are those who refuse to hear Him who speaks from Heaven. Jesus warns us of this condition:

> *And he beheld them, and said, What is this then that is written, The stone which the builders rejected, the same is become the head of the corner? Whosoever shall fall upon that stone shall be broken; but on whomsoever it shall fall, it will grind him to powder.*

Luke 20:17-18

It appears to be much more advantageous to fall upon the rock than to have the rock fall on us and to be ground to powder. God is simply using the galbanum to show us the importance of maintaining an open, teachable spirit before the Lord. The prophet Jeremiah was commissioned by God at a very young age to reach nations and kingdoms. He was told that God would put His words in his mouth and that they could root out, pull down, destroy and throw down, build and plant.

Often before God can build and plant seed in people's lives He must root out the strongholds in the mind and in the heart of man. This is the "breaking" that occurs before the "making." It is not an unpleasant process unless one stubbornly resists the hand of God. Let there be a breaking or a breakthrough in your life today. "The blessing of the Lord, it maketh rich, and he addeth no sorrow with it" (Prov. 10:22).

Pure Frankincense

Frankincense was extracted from a tree which was pierced and left all night so the sap could run. You may find yourself in the dark night of your life right now, but if you will seek the Lord in

30

this hour you'll find that He is working something wonderful in you. He is bringing forth a valuable fragrance from your life.

The word *frankincense* means "white." God will let purity flow out of you. Frankincense was one of the gifts given to the Christ-child by the wise men and represents the High Priestly ministry of Jesus as He "ever lives to make intercession for us." Those who are vessels of the Holy Spirit are to be anointed for the ministry of intercession. We are to cry out to God for the salvation of a lost and dying world and that laborers would be sent out to the harvest fields. The priestly ministry is one that goes to God on behalf of others. You're saved today because someone prayed for you; who are you praying for?

The other aspect of the priestly ministry that frankincense represents is the ministry of Christ on this earth. This occurs as we (His Body) intervene in the plans of the devil over people's lives. As intercessors, we go in between, we stand in the gap to fill in the broken part of others' walls where the devil may have entrance. This can be a very difficult ministry. The intercessor will see areas of weakness or struggle in a person's life without criticizing that one. When his prayers are answered the intercessor takes no credit or affirmation. A true priest doesn't condemn people. He delivers them by the cleanness of his own hands.

The tree from which frankincense was obtained was pierced during the night, making it useful at the darkest times of the day. In the same way, God uses the High Priestly ministry of intercession to intercept the devil's dark conspiracies. Intercession is going into the darkness and pulling people out into the light. What the devil means for evil, God can turn around for good. When the Holy Spirit "maketh intercession for the saints according to the will of God," then "we know that all things work together for good" (Rom. 8:27-28). God can turn anything into a miracle if we will fervently intercede. The increase of the anointing in our lives is directly related to the level of intercession to which we give ourselves.

Decide today to fulfill your calling as an intercessor by crying out to God for lost and dying people. Ask, and God will give you the nations for your inheritance, and the uttermost parts of the earth for your possession. There's nothing impossible to those who believe when they ask. God's anointing produces miracles, signs and wonders because with God nothing is impossible!

Chapter 3

The Corporate Anointing

The Church has been destined to work as one body before the world can be reached with God's anointing. Because the anointing and the power of God is resident within each member, we have need of one another in order to walk in "the measure of the stature of the fulness of Christ." No two members of the Body fulfill the same function or task in the same way. Every part is vital to the fulfillment of God's plan, even those parts that seem less important.

God has no pets and He has no stars. There's not "better" or "more important" in the Kingdom of God, just "specialized" and "different." There are no big I's and small U's in the work of the Lord. Everyone has a place to fit. Without each doing his part the whole Body would be lacking. "God has set the members every one of them in the body, as it hath pleased him." Even "the eye cannot say unto the hand, I have no need of thee: nor again the head to the feet, I have no need of you" (I Cor. 12:18,21).

The conditions for a corporate anointing upon the Church can be seen as three-fold. They include sanctification, oneness and unified praise unto God. These three aspects of the corporate anointing are seen explicitly during the time of the dedication of Solomon's temple:

> *And it came to pass, when the priests were come out of the holy place: (for all the priests that were present were sanctified, and did not then wait by course: also the Levites which were the singers, all of them of Asaph, of Heman, of Jeduthun, with their sons and their brethren, being arrayed in white linen, having cymbals and psalteries and harps, stood at the east end of the altar, and with them an hundred and twenty priests sounding with trumpets:) It came even to pass, as the trumpeters and singers were as one, to make one sound to be heard in praising and thanking the Lord; and when they lifted up their voice with the trumpets and cymbals and instruments of music, and praised the Lord, saying, For he is good; for his mercy endureth for ever: that then the house was filled with a cloud, even the house of the Lord; so that the priests could not stand to minister by reason of the cloud: for the glory of the Lord had filled the house of God.*
>
> 2 Chronicles 5:11-14

What made the glory fill the house? Revealed in Second Chronicles 5:11-14 are the three ingredients that brought in the glory of God to such a degree that God's priests could not even stand up to minister. These were holiness, harmony and *halel.*

Holiness

("They Were Sanctified")

This was a holy, sanctified people. *Sanctified* means "to be clean, dedicated and holy." *Holiness* means "to be separated from darkness and linked to God." Holiness is often misunderstood. It is a gift that has been imputed to us through the sacrifice of Jesus Christ, much like righteousness. When a revelation is received in the heart, it will change one's very character. Once we begin to believe that we are holy, we begin to act holy. Potentially, a born-again believer is holy, yet experientially there is a process one must work out. "Work out your own salvation with fear and trembling. For it is God which worketh in you both to will and to do of his good pleasure" (Phil. 2:12-13).

The Spirit of God is the *Holy* Spirit who lives within you. He will enable you to overcome whatever bleakness, whatever darkness, whatever corruption, whatever oppression might be attempting to invade your flesh. When the enemy comes against you, the holiness of God will rise up within you, expelling darkness. We must acknowledge the fact that God created us in His image and likeness and made us beautiful.

We were all dead in our trespasses and sins, but Christ came to make us alive. We were ugly, powerless and helpless, but He gave us the ability to overcome sin and darkness. Christ has been made unto us righteousness, and He has set us free. He has seated us with Him in heavenly places (Eph. 2:6). In Christ we are made complete, and "as He is so are we in this world."

As the Church, we are destined to walk in God's image. Filled with His glory, we are growing unto a perfect (full-grown) man, into mature sons and daughters of God (Eph.4:13; Rom. 8:19). Holiness is totally dependent on God, totally leaning on the One who lives within us...the Holy One of Israel. That's why God can use such ordinary people, for His presence in them makes them extraordinary.

When we acknowledge the fact that the Lord God is our holiness, we come face to face with Him, just as Moses did. As we set ourselves apart and sanctify ourselves we will become like

Him. We begin to know Him face to face, intimately, personally. He waits to fellowship with us so His Spirit can change us.

Harmony

("The Singers and the Trumpeters Were as One"!)

The glorious Church of the Lord Jesus Christ will be founded on people who walk in harmony. This harmony occurs when we come to know Him and see His light, love and grace. We are all ambassadors of Christ. He has given everyone a calling, a mission, a purpose. We were not just born to eat, sleep, hold a job and die. We are anointed to walk in His glory as kings and priests in Him and to come into unity with our brothers and sisters. This is so important that the gift ministries of Ephesians four, namely, apostles, prophets, evangelists, pastors and teachers, will continue "until we all come into the unity of the faith."

The Church today is much like the brothers Esau and Jacob, who warred constantly. They hated each other and were rivals in every sense of the word. The Church has so many different sects, denominations and independent groups. God is changing that. He is uniting us around the fact that He is our Father and Jesus is our brother. It is time to think beyond our personal needs to the needs of our brothers and sisters forming the entire Body of Christ.

When Jacob had his experience with God at Peniel, his life was totally changed forever. While wrestling with God, his name and nature were changed. No longer was Jacob "the deceiver," "the supplanter," "the conniver." He was now Israel, "prince of God." God has given His people a new name and a new nature of love. The name *Christian* means "Christlike." Since God's love is shed abroad in our heart by the Holy Spirit, it is our spiritual nature to be united with the whole family of God. This truth is evidenced in Jacob's life, for after he experienced God face to face, he desired to be united with his rival, Esau. In fact, Jacob's encounter with God was so powerful that at his reunion with his brother, Jacob was inspired to tell Esau that when he saw his face, it was as if he saw the face of God again.

When the members of the Church of Jesus Christ look into the light of God's Word face to face, their vision shall be changed to see their brothers and sisters as if they were the face of God.

We can't look into the brightness of the sun without our sight being blinded with light. We can't look into the Light of God's glory without our heart being changed. When all we can see is God's glory, everything looks different to us, even our brothers and sisters.

David understood the importance of both a relationship with God and relationships with others. He surrounded himself with faithful men of like precious faith. These men loved David to the point that they were willing to lay down their lives for him. Once, when the Philistines invaded their camp, David and his men were forced to take refuge in the cave of Adullam. David was thirsty and longed for a drink of water from the well of Bethlehem. Several of his mighty men overheard him express his desire. What they *did* reveals their dedication to this man of God. They broke through into the camp of the Philistines just to get David a drink of water. When David saw that his men had risked their lives just to satisfy his heart's desire, he was so touched that he poured it out as an offering of thanks to the Lord.

If men of the Old Testament could love each other so much that they were willing to die for each other, we should, through the "love that has been shed abroad in our hearts by the Holy Ghost" be able to walk in Jesus' commandment to love one another. Until this unconditional love flows among us, the world will never see the Kingdom of God manifest itself on this earth.

Halel, **Praise**

("To Make One Sound...Praising the Lord")

The Church of God will have one voice; not one voice over here and one voice over there, but one voice. And that one voice will be praising the Lord, saying, "For He is good; for His mercy endureth forever." Nothing is too difficult for our God. We must learn to radically praise Him, as an overcoming God, a God of all power whose faithfulness is to all generations. We must stop wallowing in our defeats and failures and concentrate on the fact that Jesus is an overcoming God and that He lives in us, making us the overcomers we were destined to be.

The Book of Revelation continually calls to the overcomer. Here is a sampling:

> *To him that overcometh will I give to eat of the tree of life, which is in the midst of the paradise of God.*
>
> Revelation 2:7

> *He that overcometh shall not be hurt of the second death.*
>
> Revelation 2:11

> *To him that overcometh will I give to eat of the hidden manna, and will give him a white stone, and in the stone a new name written, which no man knoweth saving he that receiveth it.*
>
> Revelation 2:17

> *And he that overcometh, and keepeth my works unto the end, to him will I give power over the nations...*
>
> Revelation 2:26

> *He that overcometh, the same shall be clothed in white raiment; and I will not blot out his name out of the book*

of life, but I will confess his name before my Father, and before his angels.

Revelation 3:5

Him that overcometh will I make a pillar in the temple of my God, and he shall go no more out: and I will write upon him the name of my God, and the name of the city of my God, which is new Jerusalem, which cometh down out of heaven from my God: and I will write upon him my new name.

Revelation 3:12

It is important to overcome. The problem is that many of us haven't learned the keys to overcoming: the blood of the Lamb, the word of our testimony and reckoning ourselves dead unto sin (Rev. 12:11; Rom. 6:11). When sin crops up in our lives and we feel ungodly, we need to take a stand and say, "I am dead to sin. It has no power over me. God has equipped me to live the overcoming life." Then we can start praising God for it along with the rest of the overcomers.

How beautiful upon the mountains are the feet of him that bringeth good tidings, that publisheth peace; that bringeth good tidings of good, that publisheth salvation; that saith unto Zion, Thy God reigneth! Thy watchmen shall lift up the voice; **with the voice together** *shall they sing: for they shall see eye to eye, when the Lord shall bring again Zion.*

Isaiah 52:7-8

The Church is beginning to lift up the voice together. We are beginning to see "eye to eye." It is time to lay aside our petty differences and reach out to the oppressed. It is time to go beyond praying for our own personal needs—my car, my clothes, my home. It is time to use our faith to pray for hurting people, lost souls, the depressed, beggars, the blind, the lame. It is time to lay

39

aside "every weight, and the sin which doth so easily beset us" and to "run with patience the race that is set before us" (Heb. 12:1).

With these three principles of the anointing in our life—holiness, harmony and praise—the Church will not be defeated. There is great power in this corporate anointing. When this truth is understood, we will be more effective in protecting the Body against the attacks of the enemy. The apostle Paul said, "To whom ye forgive any thing, I forgive also: for if I forgave any thing, to whom I forgave it, for your sakes forgave I it in the person of Christ; lest Satan should get an advantage of us: for we are not ignorant of his devices" (II Cor. 2:10-11).

What are satan's devices? According to Paul, they are unforgiveness, accusation, strife, misunderstanding, division and anything that keeps us from corporateness. Many fear this unity because they may lose their control (of something) or have to defend what they believe. What we must understand is that our fight for victory and success is not against each other.

Ephesians 6:12 says, "We wrestle not against flesh and blood." You are not wrestling against your unsaved mother, husband or boss. You are wrestling against a spirit that holds them captive. You must rise up and say, "In the name of Jesus I rebuke the forces of hell and I loose the power of God upon these people, that the angels of God would go and minister peace, help, strength, comfort, revelation and insight to them." Then love them into the Kingdom. Unconditional love will never fail!

We are not wrestling against other members of the Body, no matter who they may be. Our fight can never be against brothers and sisters in Christ. "For we wrestle...against principalities, against powers, against the rulers of the darkness of this world, against spiritual wickedness in high places" (Eph. 6:12). God wants the Body of Christ to come together. He wants the members of the Body of Christ to be in love with one another.

We have been anointed with God's power and revelation in order to help people who don't understand the Lord or may never have been taught about His goodness. God hasn't called us to make war against denominations or to straighten out everyone we disagree with. Our battle is not against people, anyway. It is against the devil. We are commanded to love people with all of our hearts.

"As we have therefore opportunity, let us do good unto all men, especially unto them who are of the household of faith" (Gal 6:10). With one heart and one soul we will radiate God's life to a dark world.

I thank God for all those who have been called into His army, no matter what denomination they are in. Our fight is against rulers of darkness, against spiritual wickedness in high places.

Wherefore take unto you the whole armour of God, that ye may be able to withstand in the evil day, and having done all, to stand. Stand therefore, having your loins girt about with truth, and having on the breastplate of right-eousness; and your feet shod with the preparation of the gospel of peace; above all, taking the shield of faith, where-with ye shall be able to quench all the fiery darts of the wicked. And take the helmet of salvation, and the sword of the Spirit, which is the word of God: Praying always with all prayer and supplication in the Spirit, and watching thereunto with all perseverance and supplication for all saints...

Ephesians 6:13-18

"Above all, taking the shield of faith..." Isn't that interesting? It is so important to have faith. It is also important to make

41

"supplication for all saints." We are to pray corporately for saints in other nations who are hurting, those who are being persecuted and who are even dying for their faith. As some of the Church sits in luxurious surroundings thinking that everything is just fine, others are suffering. God is changing that way of thinking, allowing us to feel the pain of others. The great things God has envisioned in this earth will be accomplished only as we unite together in the Spirit with the heart of our Father.

The time is coming when we will flow so beautifully together that all the world will see it and will know we are Christians.

And now, Lord, behold their threatenings: and grant unto thy servants, that with all boldness they may speak thy word, by stretching forth thine hand to heal; and that signs and wonders may be done by the name of thy holy child Jesus. And when they had prayed, the place was shaken where they were assembled together; and they were all filled with the Holy Ghost, and they spake the word of God with boldness. And the multitude of them that believed were of one heart and of one soul: neither said any of them that aught of the things which he possessed was his own; but they had all things common. And with great power gave the apostles witness of the resurrection of the Lord Jesus: and great grace was upon them all. Neither was there any among them that lacked: for as many as were possessors of lands or houses sold them, and brought the prices of the things that were sold, and laid them down at the apostles' feet: and distribution was made unto every man according as he had need.

Acts 4:29-35

The miracles recorded in the Book of the Acts of the Apostles happened because the people were "of one heart and one soul."

They rejoiced together. They wept together. They gave to each other as they faced need together. Miracles happen when God's people have one heart. The Kingdom of God is like a net (Matt. 13:47). A net is made up of many pieces woven together. When we get the vision of the Church as one Body, the glory of God which came in Solomon's day in a corporate anointing will be manifested again in our day.

After these things Jesus shewed himself again to the disciples at the sea of Tiberias; and on this wise shewed he himself. There were together Simon Peter, and Thomas called Didymus, and Nathanael of Cana in Galilee, and the sons of Zebedee, and two other of his disciples. Simon Peter saith unto them, I go a-fishing. They say unto him, We also go with thee. They went forth, and entered into a ship immediately; and that night they caught nothing. But when the morning was now come, Jesus stood on the shore: but the disciples knew not that it was Jesus. Then Jesus saith unto them, Children, have ye any meat? They answered him, No. And he said unto them, Cast the net on the right side of the ship, and ye shall find. They cast therefore, and now they were not able to draw it for the multitude of fishes. Therefore that disciple whom Jesus loved saith unto Peter, It is the Lord. Now when Simon Peter heard that it was the Lord, he girt his fisher's coat unto him, (for he was naked,) and did cast himself into the sea. And the other disciples came in a little ship; (for they were not far from land, but as it were two hundred cubits,) dragging the net with fishes. As soon then as they were come to land, they saw a fire of coals there, and fish laid thereon, and bread. Jesus saith unto them, Bring of the fish which ye have now caught. Simon Peter went up, and drew the net to land full of great fishes, an hundred and fifty and three: and for all there were so many, yet was not the net broken.

John 21:1-11

The Kingdom of God is like a net. This net enclosed one hundred and fifty-three fish, yet it was not broken. One hundred and fifty-three represents the nations of the earth that are presently ripe for harvest. Only God's net is able to enclose them all. We must join our forces together to form a mighty net that will not break or have gaps in it from pulling away from each other. The Body of Christ, as a whole, will be thrown out to all the nations of the world to preach the Kingdom of God and to draw in the harvest.

The Kingdom of God is within us. That Kingdom is the rule and reign of Christ in every specific area of life. Because the Body of Christ is the vehicle God uses to demonstrate the Kingdom rule of God on this earth, no one member of the Body can exist independently. Each member must find his place in the Body as it pleases God. When we are perfectly joined together, so that there are no holes in the net, then none that are caught will be lost!

When we insist upon being a "Lone Ranger" and keep ourselves outside the Body of Christ, we become a prey to the dangers and attacks of the enemy. When that happens, we have nowhere to turn. We need the strength and safety derived from union with the whole Body. That is why we are admonished to "not forsake the assembling of ourselves together" (Heb. 10:25).

It is not just "Jesus and Me" "On the Jericho Road." I must be "fitly framed together" with the rest of the Body (Eph. 2:21). Many don't want to pay the price of forgiveness, unselfishness, humility, kindness or things that make for peace. They flee uncomfortable situations with others to keep from being hurt and rejected. But in order to become the unified Body of Christ we must be bold to

44

forgive, to put others first and to speak the truth in love. We must strive to attain the corporate anointing.

What will it take to weave a net that will not break? It is necessary that the body of Christ demonstrate unconditional, never-ending agape love. Pray in agreement the prayer that Jesus prayed at the end of His life on earth:

> *Neither pray I for these alone, but for them also which shall believe on me through their word; that they all may be one; as thou, Father, art in me, and I in thee, that they also may be one in us: that the world may believe that thou hast sent me. And the glory which thou gavest me I have given them; that they may be one, even as we are one...*
>
> John 17:20-22

Ex 33:12-18
His Presence = the Anointing
Heb 1:3
Jn 17:22
Jn 20:21

Chapter 4

How Much of The Anointing do you want?

The Hundredfold Anointing

In this chapter we will look at the different levels of the anointing through some types and shadows found in the Word. We will see a pattern which teaches us about three progressive levels or degrees of the anointing that God has called us to walk in. Each level is attained through a growth process of maturing humility, sacrifice and obedience. Growing in the anointing is directly related to every other area of growth in God.

The Bible is faithful to teach us through these types, shadows, patterns and examples for our admonition and learning (I Cor. 10:11; Rom. 15:4; Heb. 8:5). Each believer must pass through these three levels during his progress toward spiritual maturity. Just as it is in natural growth, so it is in the spirit. Maturing always requires *change*. "For the earth bringeth forth fruit of herself; *first* the blade, *then* the ear, *after that* the full corn in the ear" (Mark 4:28). This change is essential for the Body to come into "the unity of the faith, and of the knowledge of the Son of God, unto a perfect man, unto the measure of the stature of the fulness of Christ" (Eph 4:13).

And the child grew, and waxed strong in spirit, filled with wisdom: and the grace of God was upon him.

Luke 2:40

If Jesus had to grow in spiritual things, how much more must we grow in the wisdom and the power of the Spirit? God has given us in His Word a spiritual growth chart to guide us. It is a road map of our journey in God that leads directly into a mature Christian life. It gives us godly standards by which to check our progress as we learn who we are in Christ and what He has destined us to accomplish. It is a narrow way that leads to life and there are few that find it. The words "find it" imply that one has to seek in order to obtain. Where do we seek and how do we find it?

Bow down thine ear, and hear the words of the wise, and apply thine heart unto my knowledge. For it is a pleasant thing if thou keep them within thee; they shall withal be fitted in thy lips. That thy trust may be in the Lord, I have made known to thee this day, even to thee. Have not I written to thee excellent things in counsels and knowledge, that I might make thee know the certainty of the words of truth; that thou mightest answer the words of truth to them that send unto thee?

Proverbs 22:17-21

The word for "excellent things" in Hebrew is *shalowsh,* which means "three, thrice; a triple; a triangle; a three-stringed musical instrument; a threefold measure or a general of the third rank." A literal translation of the Hebrew would read, "Have I not written thee *three* times?" Ecclesiastes 4:12 says, "a *threefold* cord is not quickly broken."

Threefold Truths

Throughout the Word of God we see this principle of "excellent things" or *threefold truths.* The pattern of spiritual maturity is

48

typified many times as three degrees or levels of God's anointing. The blade, the ear and the full corn in the ear. Thirtyfold, sixtyfold and a hundredfold. The Outer Court, the Inner Court and the Most Holy Place. The Feast of Passover, the Feast of Pentecost and the Feast of Tabernacles. The winter, the spring and the summer. The good (will of God), the acceptable (will of God) and the perfect (will of God).

Noah's ark contained three levels. The third level of the ark was according to God's instructions—*thirty* cubits high. *Thirty* is a number representing full maturity. Jesus began His ministry as a prophet at age thirty. King David was thirty when he began to reign. Joseph ruled on the throne when he was thirty. The third level of the anointing then represents full stature or maturity.

When Gideon was going into battle against the Midianites, God told him to reduce the number of the army lest Israel claim glory for itself. So Gideon told the fearful to depart, and twenty-two thousand men left. Then God told Gideon that the people were still too many, so he was to bring them down to the water (the Word) to test them there. The third group of warriors, those who passed this test, were *three hundred*. Here again, we see *three* levels of maturity, each requiring greater commitment and sacrifice. This three hundred company of Gideon's army are God's hundredfold Christians. This, no doubt, is a special group. In the Book of Judges, which is the seventh book of the Bible, in the seventh chapter, the seventh verse we read (note three 7's), "And the Lord said to Gideon, By the three hundred men that lapped I will save you, and deliver the Midianites into thine hand..."

When looking at types of the anointing oil it is interesting to note that when Mary poured the very costly oil of spikenard over Jesus' feet, Judas said, "Why was not this ointment sold for *three hundred* pence?" This shows that the price for the costly anointing is being part of the three hundred.

An example of this maturing process is the journey from outside the tent of meeting through the three gates into the presence of God in the Most Holy Place. The Tabernacle which Moses was instructed to build in the wilderness had three sections: the Outer Court, the Inner Court and the Most Holy Place. God doesn't want us to stay in the Outer Court forever. The Inner Court is great, but He doesn't even want us to stay there. He is inviting us into the Most Holy Place, where the fire of God is manifested.

We have three progressive experiences: justification, sanctification and glorification. We have three levels of diet: the milk of the Word, the bread of the Word, and the meat of the Word. There were three levels of service to God in Israel: all the people of Israel were sacred to God; the priests, however, were more deeply dedicated to serving Him; and the High Priests were even closer to God, having privileges and responsibilities that no one else had.

We have the revelation of Jesus as our Savior. We have a deeper revelation of Christ, the Anointed One. Finally, we have the highest revelation of Him as Lord. We have spiritual infants, spiritual adolescents and spiritual adults. We have thirtyfold Christians, sixtyfold Christians and one hundredfold Christians. God wants you to have the hundredfold anointing. You can have it if you are willing to accept the responsibility and pay the price. Although this anointing is costly, great honor awaits those who are willing to pay the price to obtain it.

John Wesley said, "Give me just one hundred men who love Jesus with all their hearts and hate sin with all their hearts, and we will see the Kingdom of God established in one generation." The historical record of the accomplishments of Wesley's famous circuit riders is astonishing, to say the least.

God is calling His people to a time of solemn assembly, a coming together in fasting and prayer, a time of humility accompanied by tears. If God's people will be obedient, all Heaven will break loose upon us. The main reason that Dr. Paul Cho's church in Seoul, Korea is so powerful is that it is a praying church. When you enter the building there is an audible hum of prayer. People are worshiping God and repenting of their wicked ways.

We are going to have more churches like that one, for God's churches are getting "fired up." The hot are getting hotter and the cold are getting colder, so now is the time for us to get bolder! Fire burns out the impurities and brings out the natural beauties. The refining process for gold burns off the dross, so that its true glory and beauty can shine brightly. God is preparing a pure Bride, filled with glory and power. That is our destiny. Though we haven't arrived yet, we are moving toward the hundredfold anointing.

David had three separate anointings during his lifetime. Three is a very significant number in the Bible. It is special to God, for it denotes growth and maturity.

The First Anointing

The prophet Samuel first anointed David when the future king was a lad. With that mighty anointing he killed the bear, the lion and the giant. With this thirtyfold anointing he had a measure of the Spirit and a glimpse of the Kingdom, but his vision was not totally developed. Anointed as future king, he had great potential, although the position was not attained for some time.

As the people of God, we will not stop with our potential blessing. Being born again, we may feel very safe with our "fire

51

insurance" to avoid the fires of hell, but there is so much more. We need to get excited about our future! We should be hungry for a greater anointing! Hunger is a good sign, because it is an indication that we are growing.

David had a servant's heart. He started by happily caring for his father's sheep on the hillside. There he learned to praise and worship God. Later he was brought into the palace of Saul to serve as a minstrel for the king. When you are in the first anointing it is a time of "training for reigning." You are a student of the Word. It is a place of discipleship. You are "schooling for ruling." Your hunger and thirst for more of God makes you willing, not only to closely associate yourself with anointed people such as apostles, prophets, pastors, evangelists, teachers, and prayer warriors, but to actually serve them as David did King Saul.

David looked for ways to serve the king as he developed his own great potential in God. He was teachable, faithful and well favored. Later in his life he was called "the sweet psalmist," for he had a beautiful spirit.

Before David could reach the second anointing he passed through a wilderness experience. Saul turned against him out of jealousy over his anointing, and David was forced to flee into the wilderness and remain a fugitive for many years. Saul had fallen from the glory of God and had lost his own anointing. God said to him, "I anointed you when you were little in your own sight. But when you got so high and mighty I took the crown from you" (I Sam. 15:16, paraphrased). The pride that crept into Saul when he decided that he was great opened the way for a little boy, an anointed little boy who killed bears and lions and giants, to become a king.

It seems there is always a struggle to be faced between step one and step two. Saul represents the ways of the flesh, man-made systems or the old order. David represents the new anointing or new move of the Spirit. Saul always becomes jealous of David's accomplishments. The old order hates the new because it exposes the weaknesses and traditions of its carnal thinking. The flesh and the carnal mind will always want to remain comfortable. It is that way because they are enemies to God. Romans 8:7 says, "Because the carnal mind is enmity against God: for it is not subject to the law of God, neither indeed can be." The apostle Paul also acknowledged that a war was being waged within him (Rom. 7:23). He thanked God though that He was victorious in Christ Jesus! (v. 25)

David couldn't understand why he was being hunted like an animal when he hadn't done anything wrong to Saul. But he was determined to be faithful to God and refused to "touch God's anointed" (I Sam. 24:6). If we will stay humble during times of testing, God will bring us out and take us deeper into Him.

The Second Anointing

When David assumed the position of king over Judah, he was anointed for the second time. *Judah* means "praise." Before David was crowned King of Judah, Saul died. The old ways of the flesh must die before we can go on to the second anointing. The old ways of thinking, consciousness of dead works and religious traditions must leave. The old wineskin, the outer court, the natural way of thinking must be changed by the refining fire of the Spirit.

David's second anointing represents the sixtyfold believer, baptized in the Spirit. Baptized believers love to praise God "in spirit and in truth" (John 4:23). Here believers dance before the Lord and have great liberty in worship as they fellowship with their God. David was crowned King of Judah in Hebron, which means "fellowship."

This anointing is wonderful, and many never go any further. The difference between sixty and one hundred is forty. *Forty* means "testing." To get from the sixtyfold anointing to the hundredfold anointing we will pass through some testings. Even after Saul's death, members of his family continued to make life unpleasant for David. As we grow in God, the tests don't decrease, but our ability to receive God's grace increases. The battles we face are ever greater. That is as it should be, for the prizes to be gained are ever greater. If we really mean business with God, and are willing to go all the way with Him, He will entrust His power and anointing to us for impossible victories.

David did not waver. The house of David "waxed stronger and stronger" (II Sam. 3:1). If we consistently seek the Lord, even in the midst of battle, even in the midst of the hard times, even when our own flesh is rising up against us and urging us not to go on with God, God has promised us victory. Don't be a quitter. Determine to have God's very best, come Hell or high water. God is looking for those who will wholly follow Him and make a militant change in their generation. Don't limit the Holy One of Israel (Ps. 78:41). Go for everything God says you can be!

When people first come into the ministry, many times they're not prepared for the battles. They think everything is going to be easy and wonderful and that major doors will open quickly and dramatically with hardly any struggle. But first, God must test us to see if we are faithful. He lets us first live what we will be preaching to others. Many think "ministry" is a career or vocation. Well, it's not. It's a way of life. If we try to preach what we haven't experienced, it will be shallow and stale. But if we press in during times of testing and determine to be faithful, then rejoice, for the greater anointing is coming.

Between the second anointing and the third and final anointing comes the greatest test of all. This is the transition from sixtyfold Christianity to one hundredfold Christianity. Here is the change from a spiritual adolescent to a mature adult. Between sixty and one hundred is "forty," a testing period.

Before Jesus ministered in the power of the Spirit, He received three baptisms or anointings. First, He was baptized by John in the Jordan.

Then cometh Jesus from Galilee to Jordan unto John, to be baptized of him. But John forbad him, saying, I have need to be baptized of thee, and comest thou to me? And Jesus answering said unto him, Suffer it to be so now: for thus it becometh us to fulfil all righteousness. Then he suffered him.

Matthew 3:13-15

Jordan symbolizes "death," implying that when God first anoints us for service it will require an initial death to self and dedication to His Kingdom. Second, Jesus was anointed or baptized with the Holy Spirit.

And Jesus, when he was baptized, went up straightway out of the water: and, lo, the heavens were opened unto him, and he saw the Spirit of God descending like a dove, and lighting upon him...

Matthew 3:16

After this second baptism He was led into the wilderness to be tested with the baptism into fire, the third anointing. This entrance into the baptism into fire is the transition from the sixtyfold to the one hundredfold anointing. Jesus was tested in the wilderness for a period of *forty* days.

Then was Jesus led up of the Spirit into the wilderness to be tempted of the devil.

Matthew 4:1

55

And immediately the Spirit driveth him into the wilderness.
Mark 1:12

And Jesus being full of the Holy Ghost returned from Jordan, and was led by the Spirit into the wilderness, being forty days tempted of the devil. And in those days he did eat nothing: and when they were ended, he afterward hungered.

Luke 4:1-2

It wasn't until after these three experiences that Jesus returned in the power of the Spirit to Galilee to begin His full-time ministry as a prophet.

The Third Anointing

Finally, David was anointed king over all Israel. This was his third anointing. His training for reigning had paid off! It always does. God speaks this prophetic word to those of you desiring to move into the third anointing:

I am preparing you for the coming days, says the Lord, by a hard path that will cause you to need Me. When I visit My people in revival it will prepare them for the darkness ahead. Upon the cross Christ spoiled principalities and powers. Look to Me, My Church. Appropriate My life within you. Be crucified with Christ Jesus and then you shall live. As you are willing to walk with Me and to rejoice in suffering, you will partake of My glory. Understand this and meditate on it. Meditate on this very solemnly, for the satanic persecution and the darkness shall be as great as the glory in these coming days, in order to try to turn the elect and the anointed ones from the paths that I, the Lord, have laid for them. Many shall start, but few shall be able to finish because of the greatness of the grace that will be needed to be able to endure to the end. Think not that there shall be a time free of persecution; for it shall continue from the time of your anointing until the end. You are being prepared to be *overcomers* in all things and to finish the course.

In the Song of Solomon, God reveals to us that He has a season for everything.

> *The voice of my beloved! behold, he cometh leaping upon the mountains, skipping upon the hills. My beloved is like a roe or a young hart: behold, he standeth behind our wall, he looketh forth at the windows, shewing himself through the lattice. My beloved spake, and said unto me, Rise up, my love, my fair one, and come away. For, lo, the winter is past, the rain is over and gone; the flowers appear on the earth; the time of the singing of birds is come, and the voice of the turtle is heard in our land; The fig tree putteth forth her green figs, and the vines with the tender grape give a good smell. Arise, my love, my fair one, and come away.*
> Song of Solomon 2:8-13

Some of you may be experiencing your winter. Be of good cheer. Spring and summer are coming.

The Song of Solomon reflects the love of the Bridegroom for the Bride and the Bride for the Bridegroom. Jesus' love for you is great. He won't let you go through a perpetual winter. "Lo, the winter is past." God wants to bring us through the spring and into the summertime of our lives. He wants to bring us to a place where we cease from our struggles and enter into our rest.

You may feel like you will never arrive but, believe me, God is making something wonderful of your life. He is the Potter and we are the clay. He molds us, then places us into the fire to be hardened and made useful. After the clay has been in the fire for a while, the potter takes it out and thumps on it to hear the sound it produces. If the sound is cold and hard, he puts it back in the fire. He continues this until the pot produces a lovely ringing sound. When it has that lovely ring, and it sings in the fire, it is ready to be pulled out of the fire and used for His divine glory.

God is constantly searching for mature people.

> *Because the creature itself also shall be delivered from the bondage of corruption into the glorious liberty of the children of God. For we know that the whole creation groaneth and travaileth in pain together until now.*
>
> Romans 8:21-22

All creation is waiting for the manifestation of the *huios* of God. That word *huios* is Greek and means "mature sons." We must always appreciate and be thankful for what God is doing in our lives. Remember to sing in the midst of the fire.

> *Sing, O barren, thou that didst not bear; break forth into singing, and cry aloud, thou that didst not travail with child: for more are the children of the desolate than the children of the married wife, saith the Lord.*
>
> Isaiah 54:1

God is speaking to every one of us. If you have a barren spot in your life, start singing and worshiping God. Don't sit back and count your woes. Let your mind be filled with good, lovely, pleasant, positive thoughts of God. Think about how much He loves you. Think of how He is in control of your life. See Him hovering over you like a mother hen over her chicks. Realize that He is caring for every affair of your life.

Sing in the deepest, darkest hour. Sing as Paul and Silas did in the prison. They weren't questioning God in doubt and unbelief.

They were singing His praises, thanking Him that they were worthy to suffer for His name. Those who heard them could not understand. These men were stripped, bleeding and chained in stocks. They were kept in the innermost part of the prison where rats and spiders crawled everywhere. It was filthy, unclean, cold and smelly. Yet they were singing praise to God in the midnight hour.

If you are in a midnight hour, sitting in filth and living with a bunch of rats, let God bring a sweet song of praise out of your life in the midst of it all. Let Him try you to see if you're ready to be used. Once you are ready, He will open the windows of opportunity and use you to be such a blessing that people will not be able to contain it.

David was anointed to reign over all the house of Israel. God has destined us to rule and reign with Christ. Jesus was so misunderstood in His day that many rejected His message. Even His own disciples, although they had left all to follow Him, later forsook Him.

Three of the disciples stuck close to Him: Peter, James and John. They represent those who were living in the Most Holy Place. These three were with Jesus on the Mount of Transfiguration and saw Him changed. They saw Him face to face, behind the veil. If we draw near unto Him in the Most Holy Place, we can see Him, too.

Experiencing His glory is worth any price. Don't let the enemy deceive you and make you think that something else is more important or pleasurable. Worldly pleasures last only for a short season, then they produce the ugly stench of death. When satan has used you, he'll leave you out in the cold to die. He's mad at God and wants to get back at Him, so he tries to get at God through you, knowing that you are the thing that God loves the most. Don't listen to satan's lies or get sidetracked. Don't settle for anything less than the best that God has to offer you. Strive for God's costly hundred-fold anointing.

This maturing process is like a great relay race. There were many great runners in the relay race of God. The baton (the anointing) has been passed on to many runners over the years. The Book of Hebrews lists some of them for us: Abel, Enoch, Jacob, Moses, Joshua, Rahab, Gideon, Barak, Samson, Jepthae, Samuel and the prophets. These people were not perfect, but they ran their individual laps with dedication and commitment.

> *Who through faith subdued kingdoms, wrought righteousness, obtained promises, stopped the mouths of lions, quenched the violence of fire, escaped the edge of the sword, out of weakness were made strong, waxed valiant in fight, turned to flight the armies of the aliens. Women received their dead raised to life again: and others were tortured, not accepting deliverance; that they might obtain a better resurrection: and others had trial of cruel mockings and scourgings, yea, moreover of bonds and imprisonment: They were stoned, they were sawn asunder, were tempted, were slain with the sword: they wandered about in sheepskins and goatskins; being destitute, afflicted, tormented; (of whom the world was not worthy:) they wandered in deserts, and in mountains, and in dens and caves of the earth. And these all, having obtained a good report through faith, received not the promise: God having provided some better thing for us, that they without us should not be made perfect.*
>
> Hebrews 11:33-40

Now, it's our turn! The baton of God's costly anointing has been passed to our generation. Those who have gone on before will stand

60

in Heaven's grandstands and watch those of us who run as God's last lap runners.

> *Wherefore seeing we also are compassed about with so great a cloud of witnesses, let us lay aside every weight, and the sin which doth so easily beset us, and let us run with patience the race that is set before us, looking unto Jesus the author and finisher of our faith.*
>
> Hebrews 12:1-2

The key to victory is to keep our eyes focused on Jesus. He knows how to run this race. He has not placed us in the last lap as a *lesser* runner or as a loser. The better runners are always kept until last. We are being equipped in these last days with the greater glory for a greater work than ever before in history. "The glory of this latter house shall be greater than of the former, saith the Lord of hosts: and in this place will I give peace, saith the Lord of hosts" (Hag. 2:9). God is giving us the potential to walk in a hundredfold anointing. If we see the vision we can run the race with His power and His strength. So run like Jesus will come back tomorrow—for some people, He will!

We are destined to be overcomers. God has ordained it. Paul was an overcomer, even though he lost his head for it. Peter was crucified upside down, but he overcame. They were willing to pay any price to obtain their high calling in Christ Jesus. Truly victorious people are the givers, not the takers. They are the ones who lay down their lives for others so that others may join the race. So run with all your might! Don't stop running, even if you feel exhausted. Never stop short of the mark or give up. Remember, the race is almost won! Be comforted in knowing that at the end of the race you will run right into the arms of Jesus. His words to you will be, "Well done, good and faithful servant. You ran a good race, you finished your course, now receive your victory crown of righteousness."

Part II

The People of the Anointing

The eyes of the Lord run to and fro throughout the whole earth, to shew himself strong in the behalf of them whose heart is perfect toward him.

Second Chronicles 16:9a

...but the people that do know their God shall be strong and do exploits.

Daniel 11:32b

Chapter 5

A People after God's Own Heart

God desires to entrust a people with a great anointing and much power. He is not waiting for us to become perfect before He uses us. He is simply wanting to show Himself strong to those whose hearts are yielded to Him.

The people of God are going through training in order to become a people of the anointing. If we really examine our lives, we can all find areas where our heart is not turned totally to God. The anointing, His Spirit, will only flow through people who don't resist Him. Since their spirit, soul and body has been tempered by the Lord, the anointing flows freely from them as rivers in desert places and streams in the wilderness.

The people of the anointing will reflect particular characteristics of God's heart which we will see in the following chapters.

A modern prophet of God had a vision of the Church. He saw God implanting His own heart, one tiny, beating heart, into the womb of the Church. He could both feel and see its heartbeats. It was pulsating with life. He could sense the love of the Father for this little heart, an extension of His own and of His Son's heart. It was a new heart He was placing within the Church.

As he looked he became aware that satan had many times ripped open the womb and eaten its fruit when it had been impregnated by the Lord in the past. This time the fruit was not to be stolen or destroyed, for the Father's jealousy surrounded it.

God said He would do a new thing in the Church in the coming years, placing His very character within her. This was only the beginning. God would place His love and His other fruits into the Church. The combination of fruit and gifts would be dynamic.

Sewn around the womb he saw a British flag, a German flag, an Australian flag, a Chinese flag. The flags of many nations were on this womb. The womb of the Church exists everywhere the Church of the Lord exists, and the new heart is beginning to beat in every place, all over the world. Some of the locations, he noticed, were not desirable. They were less than perfect. He saw a little scar here, a little blemish there. He felt as though he wanted to back off sometimes, uncertain whether he wanted to be joined to those people.

But the Lord told him not to worry about the flaws, not to be opinionated or judgmental, not to speak against those he might truly learn to love.

The vision changed and the womb became as that of a great queen bee. God spoke to him and said that, like the queen bee, we will drive out the drones from the Body of Christ. We will return to the place of Israel before the kings were appointed, driving out the pagan kings and the idols from the land.

He saw that God is requiring more of us all. Those who have born good fruit will be expected to bear much more. Those who have done much for God will be expected to do much more. The queen bee, the Church, has the ability to lay thousands of eggs, but she stands at this time requiring the help of many laborers. God is calling us to be those laborers and helpers. The members of the Body of Christ will be making the honey, the good word of God, for the entire world. The eggs represent new life. Wherever we go, we will give out new life and new fruit.

In the coming days we are going to see astounding things as a new outpouring of the Spirit takes place. The time has come to rise and shine, for the Lord's vision for us is about to be fulfilled. Satan will be powerless to prevent it. The jealousy of the Father is overshadowing us and He is jealous for the manifestation of His sons in the earth.

A Heart of Unbelief

Caleb and Joshua were two of the spies who were sent in to spy out the promised land. They saw giants in the land and, although they were a minority, they came back with a good report: "We are able to go and take the country" (see Numbers 13:30). Ten of the twelve spies came back with an evil heart of unbelief, saying that it could not be done. Satan came to steal God's promised word, but Caleb refused to doubt. When God speaks, we must resist doubt as we would a terrible sin—for that is what it is.

Then the children of Judah came unto Joshua in Gilgal: and Caleb the son of Jephunneh the Kenezite said unto him, Thou knowest the thing that the Lord said unto Moses the man of God concerning me and thee in Kadesh-barnea.

67

Forty years old was I when Moses the servant of the Lord sent me from Kadesh-barnea to espy out the land; and I brought him word again as it was in mine heart. Nevertheless my brethren that went up with me made the heart of the people melt: but I wholly followed the Lord my God. And Moses sware on that day, saying, Surely the land whereon thy feet have trodden shall be thine inheritance, and thy children's for ever, because thou hast wholly followed the Lord my God. And now, behold, the Lord hath kept me alive, as he said, these forty and five years, even since the Lord spake this word unto Moses, while the children of Israel wandered in the wilderness: and now, lo, I am this day fourscore and five years old. As yet I am as strong this day as I was in the day that Moses sent me: as my strength was then, even so is my strength now, for war, both to go out, and to come in. Now therefore give me this mountain, whereof the Lord spake in that day; for thou heardest in that day how the Anakims were there, and that the cities were great and fenced: if so be the Lord will be with me, then I shall be able to drive them out, as the Lord said. And Joshua blessed him, and gave unto Caleb the son of Jephunneh Hebron for an inheritance. Hebron therefore became the inheritance of Caleb the son of Jephunneh the Kenezite unto this day, because that he wholly followed the Lord God of Israel.

Joshua 14:6-14

This new heart that God is putting in the Church is a determined heart, one that is fervent and will not faint when it sees the enemy. It is a heart like that of Joshua and Caleb. While others were full of fear and unbelief, these two were determined not to give in. They were determined to finish the course. God is raising up a Joshua generation in this hour and placing His Spirit of boldness within us.

The heathen tribes which the children of Israel had to conquer in order to claim their rightful inheritance represent the works of the enemy in our own promised land today. Listed here are definitions of what some of them represent. We as a Church must go in and conquer them to possess our inheritance.

The Canaanites: This word literally means "to press down" or "to humiliate." (Oppression can come from sickness, poverty or a number of demonic circumstances.) Depression is another word we could use to define this enemy that at some time or another everyone must defeat and conquer. The anointing of the Spirit will give us victory to rise up above our circumstances. Because God's Word to us is the highest form of reality, our faith in it will bring joy and peace in believing. "Why are you cast down, O my soul? ...hope in God" (Ps. 43:5).

The Hittites: This word means "fear" or "terror." How many times have God's people missed the promised land because they were afraid? Fear is a terrible thing. It is the opposite of faith and destroys it. God says in His Word 365 times (once for every day of the year), "fear not." We need not fear, for God is with us. He will never leave us nor forsake us. He will carry us into the promised land and will protect us from the enemies we encounter there.

The Perizzites: This word means "an unwalled city" and implies a lack of discipline. These were people who dwelt in unwalled cities. Proverbs 25:28 says, "He that hath no rule over his own spirit is like a city that is broken down, and without walls." Undisciplined people are like unwalled cities; they are neither dependable nor secure. These people are up one day and down the next without any consistency. Commitment to discipline is the key that will bring the uncommitted and undisciplined into their personal promised land. As we organize our days we will present to the Lord a heart filled with wisdom. Consistent discipline over a long period of time will win the war.

The Amorites: This word means "to speak or say" and implies negative speech. Both criticism and complaining are manifestations of negative speaking. We have all been subject to murmuring at one time or another, asking God, "Why must I do this?" Murmuring kept many of the people of Israel from the promised land. We must put a watch over our mouths so that we don't sin against God in this way. Life and death reside within the power of the tongue. Discipline your mind to meditate on that which is good, true, honest, just, pure, lovely and of a good report. The opposite of criticism and complaining is thankfulness, which happens to be "the will of God concerning you." Your thanksgiving and praise to God will always drive out the enemy.

The Jebusites: This word means "to trample," and implies depression or oppression. Depression is the complete opposite of confidence and joyfulness. The garment of praise expels a spirit of heaviness. Praise silences the enemies of God which bring oppression. As wax melts in the presence of fire, so do the enemies of God fall back at His presence. In this one thing we can be confident: If God is for us, who can be against us? The Lord reigns. The devil is defeated, so let the earth rejoice!

The Midianites: This word means "strife" or "contention." Strife will paralyze and defeat our covenant relationships within our marriage, our family, our local congregations, or any body of believers. Satan's strategy is to divide and conquer. The Lord says, "Behold, how good and how pleasant it is for brethren to dwell together in unity...for there the Lord commanded the blessing, even life for evermore" (Ps. 133:1,3). During the building of the tower of Babel, the Lord had to intervene because He saw the people were as one, and He said that nothing would be impossible for them. If this was God's judgment concerning ungodly men who were one, what will happen when God's chosen ones come together, united in the Spirit and submitted to God's purposes? There will be absolutely nothing impossible for those who walk in the unity of the faith and the knowledge of the Son of God with one heart and one way.

Philistines: This word means "to wallow in the dust" and implies self-pity. The dust is what our flesh is made of. The flesh always wants pity and pampering so it can get its own way. If one is ever going to get anywhere in spiritual things, this enemy must be put to death. It is interesting to note that little David had to slay his Philistine giant also. In fact, it was his first real battle and his most glorious victory. Perhaps this tells us that this enemy is the most common and elementary to the believer. Before coming into the promised land, thoughts and feelings of selfishness must be put to death. God loves the Church, but its carnal, selfish attitude will keep Him from releasing His blessings. The faith of God will crush the enemy and his haunting lies of loneliness, hopelessness and rejection. If a thought has no hope in it, it is not of God. Cast it down, crush it under your feet and slay your Goliath!

The Moabites: This word means "against" and implies one who is against God or is rebellious. Get rid of that Moabite in your life so that you can take your promised land! If the spirit of lawlessness is allowed to rule in the Church or in an individual's life, it will bring unfruitfulness and confusion. The rebellious live in a dry land. God's Kingdom and His government bring peace without end. Submission to His voice revealed in the Word and through His delegated authority structure of apostles, prophets, pastors, teachers and evangelists will bring you into your promised land.

The Israelites did not conquer their enemies in one day. They conquered them one at a time, little by little. You can do the same with God's help.

> *And the Lord thy God will put out those nations before thee by little and little: thou mayest not consume them at once,*

lest the beasts of the field increase upon thee. But the Lord thy God shall deliver them unto thee, and shall destroy them with a mighty destruction, until they be destroyed.

Deuteronomy 7:22-23

Be patient. God will destroy your Jebusites. He will tear down your oppression. He will purge all rebellion. He will give you your promised land, by His Spirit.

When Zerubbabel was commanded to rebuild the Temple, the enemy arose to prevent him. God told him to proceed, but not in his own strength, nor with confidence in his own might. The words spoken to him have become a classic cry of God's people.

Not by might, nor by power, but by my spirit, saith the Lord of hosts.

Zechariah 4:6b

It is the working of the Spirit of God within that destroys those enemies step by step. When we speak forth the word of faith, God will confirm it with signs following. Use the sword of the Spirit that God has given you. Walk in faith and victory, knowing that everything contrary to God is a lesser power.

Beloved, think it not strange concerning the fiery trial which is to try you, as though some strange thing happened unto you: But rejoice, inasmuch as ye are partakers of Christ's sufferings; that, when his glory shall be revealed, ye may be glad also with exceeding joy.

First Peter 4:12-13

The tests of faith you are experiencing may be necessary for you to see the glory that God has prepared for you. When the devil tries to oppress you and steal the Word of God from you, know that it is a sign that God wants to do something great in your life. He wants to give you a ministry of reconciliation. The enemy is trying to prevent it from coming forth. Don't let that defeated foe deceive you. Hold your head high because, through Jesus Christ and God's Spirit, you are an overcomer.

David was a small boy, but he had a heart after God. His name means "beloved." He was God's beloved. God took him from the sheepfold and gave him a great position of authority. But David had to pass many tests. For eight or ten years he ran from Saul, living as a fugitive in the wilderness. If you will recognize it, God is working in your life too. You are defeating your giants and inheriting the promise.

Joseph went from the pit to the prison to the palace. His brothers threw him in the pit because they were jealous of his calling and dream from God and of the favor their father showed him. Are you in a pit today? Joseph called upon God, and God took him out of that pit and brought him to Egypt. He was sold into slavery, but God had a higher purpose. Joseph served faithfully as a slave and was honored by his master. Then, just when it seemed that God was working to deliver him from slavery, a terrible thing happened. He was wrongly accused, framed by Potiphar's wife, and thrown into prison. But Joseph didn't get depressed in the prison. He didn't let his gifts become dormant. He didn't stop believing God in the prison.

When Pharaoh had a strange dream, Joseph was called upon to interpret it. Pharaoh recognized that Joseph was the only one who could perform the work envisioned in the dream, so he gave him a governmental position as one of the king's trusted aids.

Queen Esther was a beautiful lady, fashioned after God's own heart. She began as a young servant girl loving and obeying God, submitting herself to His teachings and to His leadings. That's why He chose her to save her people. Powerful officials were plotting against them, but she didn't despair. She prepared herself faithfully for twelve months, and was rewarded by being chosen to be the king's wife.

In Esther 2:12, we read of Esther purifying herself for six months in the oil of myrrh, which represents the anointing oil of the Spirit. The last six months were spent bathing in sweet odors, representing the sweet perfume of Exodus 30:34-36. Esther is a type of the Spirit-filled, overcoming Church. She reflects the beauty of the Bride of Christ—courageous, submitted and anointed by God to rule and reign. We must recognize, as Esther did, that we have "come into the kingdom for such a time as this" (Esth. 4:14).

There are still many kingdoms and much land to be conquered. Take your promised land and drive out the enemies. Remember, God is on your side. Go forth in the anointing of His Spirit.

Chapter 6

A People of the Word and Spirit

And all the elders of Israel came, and the priests took up the ark. And they brought up the ark of the Lord, and the tabernacle of the congregation, and all the holy vessels that were in the tabernacle, even those did the priests and the Levites bring up.

So that the priests could not stand to minister because of the cloud: for the glory of the Lord had filled the house of the Lord.

First Kings 8:3-4,11

Many believers are still trying to serve God in David's Tabernacle, while God is trying to move us into the anointing of Solomon's Temple, the completion of David's ministry.

After the children of Israel returned to the promised land, the Tabernacle of God was set up on Mt. Gibeon. When David removed the Ark from Gibeon, he left priests there to serve. The Temple utensils were apparently left there also. Everything was left there except the Ark, which contained the presence of the Lord. It was transported to Mt. Zion. It was not until the time of Solomon, when the two were brought together again, that the glory of God fell as it had done in the wilderness.

David's Tabernacle was a place without pattern, a place of spontaneity, a place of praise and abandoned worship. There can be no doubt that God was honored there. Yet the established form and ritual were still being carried out on Mt. Gibeon. David's desire was to build a House or a Temple for the Mighty One of Israel. But he was not permitted to do so because he had been a man of war. So Solomon, a man of peace, was given unusual ability and great wealth to accomplish its building.

When it was finished, the priests and the Temple utensils were brought from Mt. Gibeon, which represents the law, the form and structure of God's House. The Ark was also brought up from David's Tabernacle, which represents the flow and spontaneity of the Spirit. Then these were united in one place. That day the glory of God manifested itself in the new Temple. It was so strong that "the priests could not stand to minister by reason of the cloud."

God is calling the Church into balance. He will combine in us the structure and order of Mt. Gibeon with the spontaneity evident on Mt. Zion. He doesn't want us to quench the Spirit, but to be a foundation or structure that will contain the flow of the Spirit. What some people call "liberty," God calls "confusion." A good example of this is the fountain pen. The ink needs the solid structure to contain it. The structure needs the ink to flow through it, or else there is nothing understandable produced from either the ink or the container. The Holy Spirit flows perfectly in the framework of the written Word.

Life is wonderful, but without structure we cannot maintain it. It's like a human body. Without the skeleton we couldn't have the muscles, the blood or the pulmonary system. It works the other way too. Nothing is worse than a bunch of dry bones. We need both the skeleton and the other elements that give life to the structure. Which is more important? They both have equal importance. Either without the other is useless.

Jesus lived by God's laws, and God wants us to live by them. They'll give us stability. If we know His Word, He can trust us with His power. The fulness of God will be achieved by combining the holiness of God with the power of God. If we want the glory to fall as it did in Solomon's Temple, we need the union of the structural foundation in the Word of God with the liberty of the Spirit and His gifts.

God wants us to be free and uninhibited, but He also wants us to be strong and discerning. We need a marriage of responsibility and intimacy. God is calling us to responsibility in this hour. We're not serious enough about this thing. It is a matter of life or death with a real Hell to shun and a Heaven too good to miss. God is calling us to accountability. This is not legalism. This is mature Christianity evidenced by a demonstration of both power and purity.

> *I indeed baptize you with water unto repentance: but he that cometh after me is mightier than I, whose shoes I am not worthy to bear: he shall baptize you with the Holy Ghost, and with fire: whose fan is in his hand, and he will thoroughly purge his floor, and gather his wheat into the garner; but he will burn up the chaff with unquenchable fire.*
> Matthew 3:11-12

John foresaw the coming of one who would have a greater baptism to offer. Yet when Jesus came, He insisted that John baptize Him first.

Then cometh Jesus from Galilee to Jordan unto John, to be baptized of him. But John forbad him, saying, I have need to be baptized of thee, and comest thou to me? And Jesus answering said unto him, Suffer it to be so now: for thus it becometh us to fulfil all righteousness. Then he suffered him.

Matthew 3:13-15

Jesus insisted that He be baptized by John in order "to fulfill all righteousness." Isn't that beautiful? Jesus didn't come to trample on all that God has done in the past.

Think not that I am come to destroy the law, or the prophets: I am not come to destroy, but to fulfil.

Matthew 5:17

By the manifestation of God's grace through Christ, the Law was fulfilled. Yet while it was still in existence, Jesus warned those who would ignore it, and called those who would walk in the ways of the New Testament to an even higher path.

For verily I say unto you, Till heaven and earth pass, one jot or one tittle shall in no wise pass from the law, till all be fulfilled. Whosoever therefore shall break one of these least commandments, and shall teach men so, he shall be called the least in the kingdom of heaven: but whosoever shall do and teach them, the same shall be called great in the kingdom of heaven. For I say unto you, That except your righteousness shall exceed the righteousness of the scribes and Pharisees, ye shall in no case enter into the kingdom of heaven.

Ye have heard that it was said by them of old time, Thou shalt not kill; and whosoever shall kill shall be in danger of the judgment: But I say unto you, That whosoever is angry with his brother without a cause shall be in danger of the judgment: and whosoever shall say to his brother, Raca, shall be in danger of the council: but whosoever shall say, Thou fool, shall be in danger of hell fire. Therefore if thou bring thy gift to the altar, and there rememberest that thy brother hath aught against thee; leave there thy gift before the altar, and go thy way; first be reconciled to thy brother, and then come and offer thy gift.

Matthew 5:18-24

The law tells us not to kill, but the Spirit takes it one step further and says, "Don't hate. Don't be angry with your brother." We fulfil the law of Christ when we are willing to bear one another's burdens (Gal. 6:2). When we get ready to obey that admonition, great glory will fall on us.

We are only beginning to see the great things that God has prepared for us. Some of us are going to be walking on water. We are going to experience the same miracles that Jesus did, that Paul did, and that many in the Church are experiencing today.

We don't have to do everything perfectly. We may make some mistakes. God's grace will be sufficient. We should cultivate the fear of God, developing a true attitude of humility, and God will bring us through. Peter "blew it" several times, but he was there on the Day of Pentecost when the fire of God fell. He preached that sermon that brought thousands into the Kingdom. Even Judas could have been used. If he hadn't given up hope and committed suicide, God would have forgiven him and used him as well as any other disciple.

Be patient. It takes time to develop a supernatural, miraculous lifestyle. We all expect to be walking in our high calling overnight.

It takes time and patience to learn God's ways and flow with God's structure. As we move into a balance between God's Spirit and God's order, we will experience the glory of a new anointing.

Chapter 7

A Faithful Bride

And Abraham was old, and well stricken in age: and the Lord had blessed Abraham in all things. And Abraham said unto his eldest servant of his house, that ruled over all that he had, Put, I pray thee, thy hand under my thigh: and I will make thee swear by the Lord, the God of heaven, and the God of the earth, that thou shalt not take a wife unto my son of the daughters of the Canaanites, among whom I dwell: but thou shalt go unto my country, and to my kindred, and take a wife unto my son Isaac. And the servant said unto him, Peradventure the woman will not be willing to follow me unto this land: must I needs bring thy son again unto the land from whence thou camest? And Abraham said unto him, Beware thou that thou bring not my son thither again.

Genesis 24:1-6

Abraham was responsible for seeking a wife for his son, Isaac. He could not go himself, so he entrusted the search to a faithful

81

servant, Eleazar. Just as father Abraham sought a bride for his son Isaac, in this day Father God is seeking a Bride for His Son Jesus. The Father has sent His Helper, the Holy Spirit, to seek and to save this anointed Bride. She will be a demonstration of three characteristics evidenced in Genesis 24.

> *And the servant put his hand under the thigh of Abraham his master, and sware to him concerning that matter. And the servant took ten camels of the camels of his master, and departed; for all the goods of his master were in his hand: and he arose, and went to Mesopotamia, unto the city of Nahor. And he made his camels to kneel down without the city by a well of water at the time of the evening, even the time that women go out to draw water. And he said, O Lord God of my master Abraham, I pray thee, send me good speed this day, and shew kindness unto my master Abraham. Behold, I stand here by the well of water; and the daughters of the men of the city come out to draw water: and let it come to pass, that the damsel to whom I shall say, Let down thy pitcher, I pray thee, that I may drink; and she shall say, Drink, and I will give thy camels drink also: let the same be she that thou hast appointed for thy servant Isaac; and thereby shall I know that thou hast shewed kindness unto my master.*

> *And it came to pass, before he had done speaking, that, behold, Rebekah came out, who was born to Bethuel, son of Milcah, the wife of Nahor, Abraham's brother, with her pitcher upon her shoulder.*

> Genesis 24:9-15

Be Willing

God's Bride will be a willing vessel. The Holy Spirit gives people a choice. He extends an invitation, saying, "I have need of you. I am reaching out My hand to you. Will you come away, My beloved, and become what I desire you to be?" The Bride always has the privilege of choosing how to respond.

Rebekah came to the well with a pitcher on her shoulder, ready to work. God's Bride is going to be a working Church. God desires that we come every day to His throne with a pitcher, ready to work, drawing water out of the wells of salvation. Our part is to be willing to do anything He wants us to do. God will never ask us to do anything that is too hard for us. We may think that it's too difficult, but His grace always is sufficient. Jesus said, "My yoke is easy and My burden is light." God's way can seem easy, for when He asks us to do a certain thing, it will always produce fruit, ability and the anointing.

Be Obedient

And the damsel was very fair to look upon, a virgin, neither had any man known her: and she went down to the well, and filled her pitcher, and came up. And the servant ran to meet her, and said, Let me, I pray thee, drink a little water of thy pitcher. And she said, Drink, my lord: and she hasted, and let down her pitcher upon her hand, and gave him drink.

And when she had done giving him drink, she said, I will draw water for thy camels also, until they have done drinking.

Genesis 24:16-19

When the request for a drink was given, Rebekah immediately complied. Some people are like goats. They answer, "But, but, but Lord..." The Lord wants sheep. They say, "Ye-e-s, ye-e-s, Lord, ye-e-s." God is looking for obedient people.

83

The Kingdom of God begins very simply as God's rule and reign in our hearts. It then proceeds to flow out of us as it influences every other kingdom that we contact. As Jesus becomes Lord over what we do, say and think, He blesses everything our hand finds to do because He is in total control over it.

Jesus preached the Kingdom of God. That Kingdom is inside us. It is experienced when Jesus becomes more important to us than anything. As we unashamedly fall in love with the Man Christ Jesus and become obsessed with His Lordship, His Kingdom blessing, inheritance and victory become ours.

Most of us do the opposite. We plan everything, then we ask God to bless our plans. He hasn't promised to bless us in our own plans. Seek God for His plan. Let Him guide and direct you. Let Him take control of your life.

Submit yourself to God. This is one of the most important keys to overcoming the enemy. We can resist the devil if we are submitted to God. If we have left Him out of our plans, we are at the devil's mercy.

> Take they our life, goods, fame, child and wife. Let these all be gone, they yet have nothing won. His kingdom now prevails.
>
> Martin Luther

Don't be fearful of submitting everything under the mighty hand of God's authority. When we submit to His authority, we walk in and reflect that authority in the earth. His Name becomes our name and His authority becomes our authority. When this happens, devils and religious people become nervous, for they are no longer in control—and neither are you!

Be Faithful

Faithfulness may be the most difficult characteristic to develop. Rebekah not only gave the servant water, she drew water for his camels. There were ten camels, and we know that camels drink a lot of water. She went back to the well over and over again until every camel was satisfied. That was a lot of work. That required perseverance and faithfulness! God is looking for faithful men and women. He is calling for faithful servants. When we come into His eternal Kingdom, may the first words we hear be, "Well done, thou good and faithful servant. Inherit the blessings I have for you."

It is in this area of faithfulness that many people have difficulty. It is easy to be willing and obedient once or twice, but what happens when God requires obedience from us as He did from Abraham, in waiting patiently many years for the promise? What if the unbelief of others postpones our receiving the promise, as it did for Caleb, who waited forty-five years before Hebron was given to him? We must always be cognizant that God is faithful. He will keep His promise.

When Abraham's servant showed up at the well that day, we can only surmise what the rest of the women were thinking. Rebekah was thinking about service. Was the man thirsty? Could she be of service to him? No doubt his camels were thirsty, as well. She didn't know what her reward would be; she just wanted to be of service. But God is a rewarder of those who diligently seek Him (Heb. 11:6). To be the Bride that God is seeking, we must be like Rebekah. We must keep watering those camels, because the reward is coming!

Many people like the promises, but don't care for the conditions. They want to reign with Christ, but aren't willing to suffer.

If we suffer, we shall also reign with him...
Second Timothy 2:12

Many portions of Scripture speak of faithfulness and diligence. For example, we read the following in the Book of Proverbs:

The hand of the diligent maketh rich.
Proverbs 10:4

The hand of the diligent shall bear rule.
Proverbs 12:24

The thoughts of the diligent tend only to plenteousness.
Proverbs 21:5

He that diligently seeketh good procureth favour...
Proverbs 11:27

Seest thou a man diligent in his business? he shall stand before kings; he shall not stand before mean men.
Proverbs 22:29

Rebekah was not watering the camels to gain a reward, but because she wanted to bless that man. Serve Jesus faithfully. Give to Him with no desire for reward, and you will get the greatest reward of all.

The king's favour is toward a wise servant...
Proverbs 14:35

He that waiteth on his master shall be honoured.
Proverbs 27:18

A faithful man shall abound with blessings...
Proverbs 28:20

God blesses and anoints faithful people. Zadok was a faithful priest during the time of Saul and David. On three different occasions, he had major decisions to make about following the Lord.

David and Saul were in mortal combat while Zadok stood on the sidelines watching. Saul represented the old order and David the new. Saul was a proud and jealous man, given over to rebellion and pride (although he was God's anointed). David was a man after God's own heart. Because Saul exalted himself, God eventually took his mantle from him and gave it to David.

The first decision Zadok had to make was whether to follow the old order or the new, a choice with which we are all faced. Will we follow tradition or the anointing? Will we do things out of pride and as they have always been done? Or will we be daring and follow new paths? God is always moving on and doing new things. The paths of our ancestors may have been adequate for them, but God is continually revealing new truths to His Church. We must have ears to hear and establish ourselves in present truth.

> *Behold, I will do a new thing; now it shall spring forth; shall ye not know it? I will even make a way in the wilderness, and rivers in the desert.*
>
> Isaiah 43:19

Zadok saw the anointing on David and chose to follow him rather than Saul. He chose to pay the price for the costly anointing.

Later Absalom, David's third son, rebelled and attempted to overthrow his father as king. Zadok prayed and asked God to show him which man to back. If Absalom were God's man, Zadok was ready to support him. God showed Zadok that Absalom was rebellious and told him not to follow the youth. Zadok obeyed and chose to be faithful to David.

Zadok made a decision that every one of us must make. Will we support the popularity of a personality or will the principles of

God become a priority over the man? Many false prophets will arise in the last days, performing lying signs and wonders to deceive even the elect. We must become fruit inspectors, not idol collectors. Let the Word of God and the fruit of the Spirit be your guides. Zadok chose principle over personality. We must do the same.

The final test for Zadok came when David had grown old. Adonijah, another of David's sons, rose up and tried to take his father's throne by force. Allegiance to Adonijah might have meant instant promotion for the priest. When Zadok prayed about the matter, however, God told him He hadn't chosen Adonijah and that he should remain faithful to David. Zadok obeyed and waited on his ministry. Because he remained faithful to the Lord and to the Lord's chosen, God promoted Zadok. When Adonijah's flame died just as quickly as it has risen, the two faithful friends, David and Zadok, remained together—side by side, hand in hand. Finally, as David lay dying years later, he said to his friend, "Zadok, you will be the High Priest in Solomon's administration." He was serving when the Presence of the Lord filled the Temple in greater glory than had ever been seen before on the face of the earth. Zadok's faithfulness was rewarded.

Faithfulness is a test we all face regularly. Will we remain faithful to God, waiting upon the Lord's timing in ministry? Or will we give way to pride? God is giving us the opportunity to have a new heart, to be faithful. Zadok chose to wait upon God for promotion and not to secure it by the arm of the flesh.

Esther was chosen because of her faithfulness. When her people were in danger, she could have looked to the good of her own position and forgotten about them. But she would not, even if it cost her life. "If I perish, I perish," she said (Esth. 4:16). "If I die,

I die." She walked into the king's private chamber and requested that he deliver her people; and she prevailed!

God knew David would be a good king because he had been a faithful shepherd, willing to risk his own life for the good of his sheep. Joseph was faithful in slavery and in imprisonment. God knew he could be trusted with authority as second in command in Egypt.

God is still looking for faithful people. Like Rebekah, keep watering those camels. Like Joseph, keep believing, even in your prison dungeon. Keep preparing yourself to rule and reign in Kingdom authority and responsibility. God is a Rewarder. When He has need of you, He will call you. He'll extend to you His right arm of power—His costly anointing. Be prepared to receive it, for it awaits all those who will dedicate themselves to faithfulness.

Chapter 8

A Hidden People

The pathway to a life of anointing in the Spirit is the pursuit of continual hiddenness with the Lord. This hidden life in God means ultimate death to soulish and fleshly motivations. It means doing what we do for no other reason than to please God and obey His will. The source of all strength, significance and spiritual power comes from a history of seeking God in "the secret place." It is a personal, intimate relationship with the Almighty that imparts wisdom, character and motivation to a special group of individuals, "a hidden people."

> *Take heed that ye do not your alms before men, to be seen of them: otherwise ye have no reward of your Father which is in heaven. Therefore when thou doest thine alms, do not sound a trumpet before thee, as the hypocrites do in the synagogues and in the streets, that they may have glory of men. Verily I say unto you, They have their reward. But when thou doest alms, let not thy left hand know what thy right hand doeth: that thine alms may be in secret: and thy*

Father which seeth in secret himself shall reward thee openly.

And when thou prayest, thou shalt not be as the hypocrites are: for they love to pray standing in the synagogues and in the corners of the streets, that they may be seen of men. Verily I say unto you, They have their reward. But thou, when thou prayest, enter into thy closet, and when thou hast shut thy door, pray to thy Father which is in secret; and thy Father which seeth in secret shall reward thee openly.

Moreover when ye fast, be not, as the hypocrites, of a sad countenance: for they disfigure their faces, that they may appear unto men to fast. Verily I say unto you, They have their reward. But thou, when thou fastest, anoint thine head, and wash thy face; That thou appear not unto men to fast, but unto thy Father which is in secret: and thy Father, which seeth in secret, shall reward thee openly.

Matthew 6:1-6,16-18

Hidden ones stay away from the limelight. Because hidden ones are not trying to be seen, most people never know that they are those who make the church successful. Most people have no idea that these handle the important assignments in the Kingdom of God. Hidden ones have the anointing and spiritual authority because they get the work done well without needing any recognition. They are confident in who they are and in He whom they serve.

While many are looking for career positions or promotions in ministry, hidden ones are looking to please the Lord. The end-time people of God must develop a history of hiddenness with Him or they will go the way of the world's system. "That which is born of the flesh is flesh; and that which is born of the Spirit is spirit" (John

3:6). If we are going to do the things of the Spirit, we must live our lives in the Spirit. It is necessary to abide in "the secret place" of the Most High, for that is the place of secrets. That is where hidden ones find their joy and contentment. It is where the costly anointing can be found.

Characteristics of Hiddenness

A primary characteristic of hiddenness is *servanthood.* God gives a special anointing to those who are dedicated to serving others. The word *minister* literally means "one who serves." There is no higher calling than to be a servant. Jesus even said that the servant was "the greatest of all." Any anointing that God gives is always dependent upon one's first being a servant.

Many servants of God lose the anointing after awhile because they stop serving and demand to be served. Because of some title or position they think they no longer need to "waste" their time helping unimportant people. But Jesus never thought anyone for whom He died was unimportant. He doesn't think of serving as a temporary hardship to be resigned once a higher status is achieved. Jesus said, "Ye know that the princes of the Gentiles exercise dominion over them, and they that are great exercise authority upon them. But it shall not be so among you: but whosoever will be great among you, let him be your minister; and whosoever will be chief among you, let him be your servant: even as the Son of man came not to be ministered unto, but to minister, and to give his life a ransom for many" (Matt. 20:25-28).

We might be surprised at the Marriage Supper of the Lamb. When we expect to see Jesus at the head table, we will see Him behind us, pouring us a glass of water. The Guest of honor will be serving. Evidence of this is found in Luke 12:37. "Blessed are those servants, whom the lord when he cometh shall find watching: verily I say unto you, that he shall gird himself, and make them to sit down to meat, and will come forth and serve them." He has a servant's heart, and He is looking for a people who have the same.

We need to get our thinking straightened out. We glorify idols. God glorifies servants. We desire stardom. He desires humility. He seeks those who have developed a hidden devotional life. The aggressiveness He seeks is very different from the aggressiveness we see in the world. His is a selfless aggressiveness, seeking to serve others rather than exalting self.

A second characteristic of a hidden people is a history of *devotional prayer* and *intercession*. The literal place of hiddenness comes as a result of communication with the Lord, both in personal prayer and in intercession for others. The life of an intercessor is a life of spiritual warfare. Prayer is where the battle is won or lost. One who never enters into the act of prayer never enters the act of spiritual warfare. It is in prayer that we see the magnitude of our weakness, but it is also in prayer that we receive the grace to overcome.

A hidden people accomplish their assignments from the Lord in prayer before presuming to know how to accomplish them in their natural strength. This means their work's success or failure is based simply upon the answer to prayer. Because of the faith-fulness and humility of their prayers, God uses them as a vehicle to bring His will to pass in this earth.

Two people like this were Simeon and Anna. They were hidden, humble people. They had a vision and a dream, but lived a hidden life of devotion to God. When the time was right they emerged, and God revealed them to the world. Simeon and Anna were probably the first ones in Jerusalem to recognize who Jesus really was. These two had been called of God to pray for the coming of the Messiah to the earth in God's appointed time. They had been looking for Him and praying for Him so long that they miraculously recognized Him when His parents brought Him into the Temple.

God is bringing hidden people out of the prayer closets of life. They have been with Jesus and experienced His presence. They know Him, and because they have been fellowshipping with Him, the beautiful character of the Lord has been developed in them.

Jesus Christ was the perfect Intercessor on this earth. In fact, He still lives to make intercession for us in Heaven. His death on the cross was the highest act of intercession ever accomplished. Devotional prayer produces the faith, hope and love necessary for a life of intercession, which includes intercessory prayer.

Intercession is more than words. As the Scripture says, "the kingdom of God is not in word, but in power" (I Cor. 4:20). An individual who desires to be an ambassador of Christ, reconciling the world to God, will experience a tremendous anointing. Intercession—especially intercessory prayer—is often a thankless job. Although it is the most hidden ministry, the anointing will not flow without it. This bears repeating. The degree to which we intercede is the degree to which we will experience the anointing. The anointing is not for self-promotion, but for others' benefit. Intercession can only abide in a selfless heart hidden in God.

A third characteristic of hiddenness is that of *forgiveness* or graciousness. When we become hidden in God and dead to self, we are no longer "touchy." If someone rubs us the wrong way, we don't lose our salvation. People can stomp on us and run over us and it doesn't matter. You can't offend a dead man. Dead men don't care if they get their own way, as long as God gets His.

The Kingdom of God is built on relationships. Anything that hinders relationships hinders the building of the Kingdom. A life of hiddenness in God causes our relationships to flourish because we are gracious and forgiving.

It's easy to find fault and to make judgments, but to forgive and cover our brothers' mistakes requires the love of God. Those who are hidden in God have seen just how much God has forgiven them. Those who are forgiven much love much. As carriers of His grace, we have the power to bind people with unforgiveness or to loose them with His mercy (Matt. 18).

Jesus, our pattern of hiddenness, continually reached out with grace and forgiveness to lost and hurting people. He also confronted the religious leaders of His day, the Pharisees, who were neither hidden nor forgiving. They were the epitome of hypocrisy, displaying only an outward show of obedience to rules and possessing no inward qualities of grace and mercy. Jesus said these hypocritical Pharisees were of their father, the devil.

Those walking in the power of forgiveness will be walking in the power of the anointing. The way God has chosen to heal and deliver the human race is through forgiveness. Without this aspect of hiddenness in our lives, the world will never know the true character of the Savior or the good news of salvation.

A fourth characteristic of a hidden person is that of *compassion.* Compassion is foundational, affecting all of our motivations and decisions. When the love of God is the driving force empowering us for service, we will have the anointing to move in and demonstrate the ministry of Jesus. We can see by Jesus' earthly ministry that He was continually "moved," or motivated by compassion. The results were miraculous. That is why we are called to live in the anointed realm of the miraculous.

Compassion comes from a life of hidden fellowship and communion with the Father. When we experience His love and forgiveness we can then demonstrate it to others. The degree to which we have received and acknowledged God's forgiveness toward ourselves is the degree to which we can give and minister love to others. When we dwell in the throne room of His grace, our lives will reflect His love and grace in relationship to others. That is when the anointing can flow through us in purity and power.

If a man say, I love God, and hateth his brother, he is a liar: for he that loveth not his brother whom he hath seen, how can he love God whom he hath not seen? And this commandment have we from him, that he who loveth God love his brother also.

First John 4:20-21

The hidden ones have spent time with God, getting to know Him and experiencing His love so that they can love their brothers. Loving and knowing God through relationship is the only way we can be anointed to love others.

A consistent abundant life in God is not usually displayed in great outward manifestations of success. It is a steady walk of victory over the daily temptations of depression, bitterness, apathy and lukewarmness. With God, bigger does not always mean better. God has a way of looking past the exterior, straight into the hidden man of the heart. The secret to living in God's anointed, abundant life is to have a hidden relationship with Him. Many of God's people have walked with God in the desert places, where they have had not man nor beast to feed them. Even as John the Baptist, the forerunner of the Lord, knew Him in the wilderness, so many of God's anointed end-time ministries will come forth from the wilderness.

For ye are dead, and your life is hid with Christ in God.

Colossians 3:3

God desires that we be hidden in the character of a devout life, knowing that Jesus is all that we need to make us happy. We don't need to be noticed. We don't need to be in the spotlight. The Holy

Spirit is the One who needs to be manifest. If we are not hidden in God and do not have the heart of a servant, we will not be qualified for this end-time anointing. Remember, one of the ingredients in the anointing oil was "frankincense," which represented purity of character. It came from a tree pierced during the night and reveals a life of hiddenness in God through prayer. Those who cultivate this hidden and humble prayer life shall arise from the secret place as a fragrant, sweet aroma to those they touch.

Hidden people are not affected by the corruption of life around them. Circumstances do not affect them. They cannot be moved. They are like trees planted by a river, having deep roots. They are not affected by lust, adultery, fornication, backbiting, strife or anger, but are firmly established upon the Rock of Christ. Self-pity, ambition and selfish desires do not move them. Winds of doctrine do not sway them.

God knows where we are. If we are willing to live a devotional life in that back closet, He is going to promote us. God is looking for a devotional people, a people of deep character. He is looking for those hidden qualities of the heart.

God is shaking the nations. He is shaking the shakable, removing the removable. He wants to make His people immovable and unshakeable. He wants to make us like a rock in the face of the devil's attacks. The shaking which has taken place in recent years in the Church has brought forth the hidden, the humble.

Whose voice then shook the earth: but now he hath promised, saying, Yet once more I shake not the earth only, but also heaven. And this word, Yet once more, signifieth the removing of those things that are shaken, as of things that are made, that those things which cannot be shaken may remain. Wherefore we receiving a kingdom which cannot be moved, let us have grace, whereby we may serve God

*acceptably with reverence and godly fear. For our God is
a consuming fire.*

Hebrews 12:26-29

The measure of our hiddenness will be revealed by our humility. This will cause us to do what God wants us to do when and how God wants us to do it. We will be hidden by representing the authority of the Lord rather than by substituting our own way of doing things for His ways. When we choose to do things our own way, we are no longer hidden with His wisdom and glory.

*Thus saith the Lord, Let not the wise man glory in his
wisdom, neither let the mighty man glory in his might, let
not the rich man glory in his riches...*

Jeremiah 9:23

Pride is a terrible thing. It is a destroyer of the soul. God is looking for a humble people who recognize their constant need of Him. A precious anointing awaits a hidden and humble people.

Chapter 9

A Prophetic People

There is a call going out in this hour for a people who will hear, speak and demonstrate the desires and purposes of God. He seeks a people who will not compromise in the face of all resistance or temptation to quit, but will press in and prevail! These people are provoking, persuasive and very prophetic. These are they for whom the Lord searches and seeks and from whom the devil runs and recoils. There are many descriptive terms for this remnant, this Bride, this Elijah Church. One thing is certain, though: They are part of God's plan. They are a prophetic people.

> *Behold, I will send you Elijah the prophet before the coming of the great and dreadful day of the Lord: and he shall turn the heart of the fathers to the children, and the heart of the children to their fathers, lest I come and smite the earth with a curse.*

Malachi 4:5-6

When God is about to do a new thing in the earth, He always shares His secrets with His prophets (Amos 3:7). They are then responsible to sound the trumpet, delivering a message to waken the mighty men to war.

An example of this is a powerful prophecy that was delivered a few years ago through Pastor Rod Parsley from Columbus, Ohio. God delivered this word to wake His Church from a spiritual stagnancy and to get it ready for a new anointing coming upon the earth. The prophecy reads as follows:

For the day of the prophet is upon you, says the Lord—the day, not of man-made prophets, but of My prophets. Have you not read in My Word and gained understanding that never a greater prophet lived than John the Baptist? My forerunner has gone before Me, and it is time for My forerunner again. Upon My first advent into this earth I sent My forerunner with an explicit message. I would have you to know that I am no respecter of persons and, as I sent My forerunner before Me that day, so will I send My forerunners this day. I would have you know that it is no different in this day. They shall come forth not from those areas that you would assume, even as John came not forth from Jerusalem. John came forth from the wilderness. My forerunners shall not come from ivory palaces. They shall not come from schools of higher learning. They shall come forth from My presence, where they have walked with Me in the wilderness, where there has not been man nor beast to minister unto them. I would not have their message defiled, nor would I have their message marred by mere mortal men. For I the Lord your God shall speak by My Spirit unto them. They shall come forth eating locusts and wild honey, and by that I would say unto you that they will have no dependency upon the world. They will not depend upon man or organizations. They shall not depend upon anything but Me to sustain them, for I, the Lord your God, have them right now in the wilderness. I have them in the back places of the desert and I am feeding them with manna from heaven. I am sustaining them by My breath and I am breathing on them afresh, for it is almost time for their demonstration. When they come forth, hear My voice in their words, and gain understanding from what I shall say. For I, the Lord, shall bring them forth and, because they depend on no man, their voice shall not be marred. Because they depend on no organization, they shall speak but what I give them to speak.

But know this, their message shall not be what many have thought, for they have come not in enticing words of man's wisdom, but in demonstration of power. And know this, that the eye of the Lord is in their head, the voice of the Lord is in their mouth, My hearing is in their ears, and they shall see what I see.

By this know that they shall receive the first part of the message. Even as the message of John coming forth out of the wilderness was "Repent," so shall the message of My prophet this day be. They shall not be as many of you have desired, ladling all the glitter of My Kingdom upon you, for My message is one of love and humility. Though it sounds a harsh message, the message of repentance is actually the greatest message of love that I can give to My people. The message of repentance shall bring refreshing from the presence of My Kingdom.

As the prophets bring forth that message, hearken. As they say, "repent of idolatry," and as they burst your idols and as they expose even your sin, as John the Baptist exposed the sin of those in Jerusalem, so shall

103

you be quick to repent. I desire to send refreshing, but first must come repentance. As you repent you shall feel the winds of refreshing by My Spirit. The latter rain shall ride upon the wings of repentance. When I hear your voice crying unto Me, I will blow the spirit of refreshing upon you and then you shall be restored. In the final hour, I will restore healing power to your hands.

Wait until you hear the anthem ringing from the prophets, for I am a great God and greatly to be praised. Refreshing and restoration shall come, and the world shall come to you. In the restoration move you shall receive what I call "promise." Repentance shall bring refreshing and refreshing, restoration. There is left but one phase for My prophets to speak, which is the proclamation of My return.

So repent, and I shall refresh you; and then shall be the restoration of all things and finally My return. But I cannot return unless My way is paved, and I cannot pave My way until the prophets speak for Me. The sound of their hoof beats are nigh at hand. Listen well. You have walked so much in the flesh that it has been hard for you to discern really what comes from My Spirit. But I will teach you. I will tell you. I have My prophets in the wilderness, but the wilderness gate is open and the prophets are nigh at hand!

Prophets are not always popular people. They are pioneers and catalysts. Often they are like steam rollers in that they are slow in coming, but you can see where they've been. When looking at a prophet in comparison to army rank and order, a prophet would be like the big bombers. They throw the stuff that shocks and jars people just enough to get them to think differently. Often they have been trained for many years for one particular season or event in God's Kingdom.

Jeremiah was very young when he was called to be a prophet. He was a shy and retiring individual with a meek spirit. God called him to be His mouthpiece, "to separate the precious from the vile." Initially, Jeremiah resisted the call because of his timid nature. God has always delighted in using those the world would never envision as prophets, for after God anoints them they become like Jeremiah—obedient and faithful. God doesn't choose the noble of this world. He delights in using the foolish things of this world to confound the wise (I Cor. 1:26-27).

Jeremiah obeyed God and became a powerful witness to the nations. The challenge has been sent to the Church. God is restoring the prophetic and apostolic ministries in this hour. He is raising up a people who will walk with a prophetic voice and speak by the spirit of prophecy.

There are many reasons why the prophetic word of the Lord must be brought forth today. Here are seven basic functions of a prophetic ministry:

1. *The prophetic ministry causes people to see their need of God.* Jesus taught in the Beatitudes that "the poor in spirit" would receive the Kingdom of Heaven (Matt. 5:3). They who mourn would be comforted, He continued. The meek would inherit the earth. Those who hungered and thirsted after righteousness would be filled (vs. 4-6). Prophetic ministry provokes and stimulates people to seek the Lord, putting Him first. It reveals the condition of the heart, making men turn from other sources to the ultimate Source—Jesus. When it takes something beyond the work of the cross and the Person of Jesus to make people happy, there is a weakness in them. This weakness will be revealed through the ministry of the prophet.

The hope that the prophetic ministry brings forth is the potential of a spirit to spirit relationship with the Lord. The basic needs of man have been designed to be fulfilled by allowing Father God to be Provider and the Holy Spirit to be Teacher. Most people function on a second-hand relationship with God, one that is handed down from a parent, teacher or pastor. This may be adequate for new babes in Christ, but maturity demands confronting the Lord in a face to face experience.

2. *The prophetic ministry brings fresh revelation to God's people.* God promised to build His Church "upon this rock," the solid foundation of revealed knowledge. The gates of Hell cannot prevail against the revelation God plants deep within our hearts. When God has revealed truth directly into an area of our lives, no one can persuade us to believe differently. The prophetic ministry confronts us at that point where we don't seek God for a direct encounter with Him and where we are comfortable with what we knew in the past.

The children of Israel, for example, had to follow the cloudy pillar in order to experience God's presence. This presence provided food, heat, protection and the essentials for survival. When the cloud moved, they had to pack up their camp and move to the next location. In the same way, when God's Spirit moves today we need to follow the cloud and not the crowd! God teaches His Church "line upon line, precept upon precept." God never retracts revelation; He only builds upon former revelation.

Those in the "comfort zone" of Christianity will not receive fresh revelation. Wanting to store up a week's worth of manna on Sunday so as to not have to gather it from Monday through Saturday, they will find, like the Israelites, that their Sunday manna has turned smelly and wormy after one day.

3. *The prophetic ministry purifies the Church.* It is called to confront and expose idolatry in our hearts. Idolatry causes jealousy and envy among us. It makes something other than God (eg., programs, doctrines, people, positions or possessions) more important to us. Idolatry causes us to give honor to something other than Jesus and His position or program. This idolatry (a focus other than Jesus) is being seriously confronted by prophetic ministry today. The spirit of Elijah confronts us primarily in our relationship to God. It says, "How long halt ye between two opinions? if the Lord be God, follow him: but if Baal, then follow him." The response is many times still the same as it was in Elijah's day: "And the people answered him not a word" (I Kings 18:21).

The prophetic ministry of Jesus is seen as He confronted the religious leaders of His day. Once He visited the Temple at Jerusalem. The Bible says that He "looked round about at all things" (Mark 11:11). The next day Jesus came back, went into the Temple and cleansed it of all idolatry and uncleanness. In the same way, the prophetic ministry operates as a seer and a watchman in the Church. In recent days the Lord has been looking at our temples (individual and corporate) and in many cases has come to cleanse it. Just as He cleansed the Old Testament Temple, Jesus is doing some house cleaning in the Church in order to make it "a house of prayer." He is not at all interested in a den of compromise.

The prophetic ministry typified in Jesus is not commissioned to be a critical judge, pointing the finger at every short-coming existing in the Body. The ministry functions as a discerning eye with the intent to exhort and stimulate the Body to good works. Since the Temple (the Body of Christ) is to be a house of prayer, any compromise will be discerned by the eye of the prophet and necessary instruction will be given. Sometimes this instruction seems so dramatic that it shakes people out of their complacency into obedience. Jesus gave this type of instruction, armed with a scourge of small cords, overthrowing all the tables of the money changers (John 2:15). Usually this kind of teaching is given to the dull of hearing.

Most of the time the prophetic ministry will call people to enter into the purity of prayer and the knowledge of the victory that has been won in Jesus. The purity that the prophetic ministry addresses aids the Church in reckoning the old man as crucified with Christ, defeating the sin that so easily stops us from Kingdom demonstration.

4. *The prophetic ministry brings oneness to the Church.* One of Jesus' last requests in His high-priestly prayer was for unity, "that they all may be one; as thou, Father, art in me and I in thee, that they also may be one in us" (John 17:21). We are destined to this kind of oneness just as surely as the Father and the Son are one. A prophetic spirit will deal strongly in relationships and the work of God's Spirit unifying the Church.

Romans 12:18 says, "If it be possible, as much as lieth in you, live peaceably with all men." A peacemaker is one who seeks to build relationships. He is not interested in unity for the sake of unity, but in oneness for the proclamation of Jesus Christ as Lord and Savior. The prophetic ministry is designed to work together with the apostles, pastors, teachers and evangelists "until we all come into the unity of the faith." The insight and instruction a prophetic ministry can give to a church is invaluable, but the spirit of the prophets must be submitted to those in authority for God's blessing to be present. In God's order, prophetic ministries will work with the other ministry gifts. Prophets will not compete, but will compliment each other, thinking of others more highly than themselves. A true prophetic ministry will respect pastoral authority and church relationships, not seeking to gather their own following apart from church structure.

5. *The prophetic ministry demonstrates both the fruit of the Spirit and God's gifts through signs and wonders.* The training of the prophet may take a period of many years. This ministry will experience many things in order to develop the character of Christ. This character is a reflection of the image of Jesus and is demonstrated through the fruits of His Spirit. As forerunners they will walk through a multitude of experiences firsthand in order to teach the ways of God to the Church. The character of Christ in them, is essential for it is a criteria by which they are to be judged. "Beware of false prophets, which come to you in sheep's clothing, but inwardly they are ravening wolves. Ye shall know them by their fruits. ...Wherefore by their fruits ye shall know them" (Matt. 7:15-16,20).

The gifts of the Spirit that will be evidenced in a prophetic ministry are primarily the revelation gifts: word of knowledge, word of wisdom and discerning of spirits. Because of the nature of the calling, it will also be accompanied by the vocal gifts: tongues, interpretation of tongues and prophecy. Visions and dreams are also common to this ministry.

6. *The prophetic ministry brings a standard of judgment to the unbelieving world.* Jesus said that the basis for judgment upon the world in the final day would be the words He speaks (John 12:47). Jesus is the Word, therefore Jesus is the standard by which the world will be judged. All those who don't receive the forgiveness of the cross of Jesus Christ will receive condemnation for their disobedience. The Church is made up of all those who by faith in the blood of Jesus have been cleansed

from all unrighteousness. "But when we are judged, we are chastened of the Lord, that we should not be condemned with the world" (I Cor. 11:32).

This standard of judgment goes beyond receiving our forgiveness to becoming a representative or ambassador of Jesus Christ. The Church must be a declaration, a living epistle to the world, of God's righteousness and holiness. True, God will judge the world by the Man Christ Jesus.

> *Because he hath appointed a day in the which he will judge the world in righteousness by that man whom he hath ordained; whereof he hath given assurance unto all men, in that he hath raised him from the dead.*
> Acts 17:31

But right now He lives in each member of His Church on earth. The idea of Christ living in people and therefore making them special is fearful to some, particularly devils. Satan is not afraid of people, he's afraid of God's authority. Any time God brings a revelation of the authority of the Church, the devil either counterfeits it or persecutes it through religious spirits in the Church. "Do ye not know that the saints shall judge the world? and if the world shall be judged by you, are ye unworthy to judge the smallest matters?"(I Cor. 6:2)

It is time for the Church to yield to the greater One who dwells inside them, to live by every word that proceeds out of the mouth of God, to allow the anointing that is resident in them to come forth as "the light of the world" and "the salt of the earth." The Church is to be the standard for the world to follow, not the reverse! When we rise up to lead, the Church will finally be that witness that the world needs to see Jesus.

Jesus said, "The words that I speak unto you I speak not of myself," and "he that hath seen me hath seen the Father" (John 14:9,10). This reveals an obedience that produced an example for everyone to follow. He came to save, not to condemn. Those who refuse to believe, however, bring condemnation upon themselves. Every man has that choice.

7. *The prophetic ministry prepares the Bride of Christ —the glorious Church.* This preparation is a washing of water by the word to remove spots, wrinkles and blemishes, while giving great comfort to the Church in the glorious hope of Jesus' second return. Titus 2:12-13 encourages us, "Teaching us that, denying ungodliness and worldly lusts, we should live soberly, righteously, and godly, in this present world; looking for that blessed hope, and the glorious appearing of the great God and our Saviour Jesus Christ..."

The plan of God's heart is to return for a people who are mature and have become mighty in spirit in this present world. Jesus is returning—but not for a baby in diapers. He is returning for a glorious Church, a beautiful Bride without spot or blemish. This Bride is wearing something other than a lovely dress and veil. She has on a pair of combat boots to enforce the Bridegroom's commands. Jesus is visualized in Scripture as a Lion and as a Lamb. The Church triumphant will not only reflect the gentle spirit of a lamb, but the ferocious might of a lion. The prophetic ministry challenges God's people to step out of infancy and into a state of responsibility. Jesus, referring to this responsibility in a parable, said, "Occupy until I come." Occupy is a military term, meaning "to possess by force." "And from the days of John the Baptist until now the kingdom of heaven suffereth violence, and the violent take it by force" (Matt. 11:12). God is raising up a people who will demonstrate Kingdom power over the forces of evil.

111

In order to accomplish this task there will be an increase in the grace of God. This will cause an increase of both our expression and experience in praise, worship and prayer. These are vital tools of the prophetic ministry that will bring a stronger sense of the presence of God. The ministry of the watchman (the intercessor) and the minstrel are to carry a mighty prophetic anointing. The psalmist ministries, of which there are three types, are of great importance to this prophetic anointing. The Davidic pattern in the Old Testament symbolizes these three types of music ministries (I Chron. 25:1-5). Asaph speaks of the leader of praise, worship and the arts. Jeduthun represents the teacher of these functions. Heman gives us the prophetic word of the Lord in music. All of these ministries functioned with a prophetic anointing as they either sang or played their instruments. "Moreover David and the captains of the host separated to the service of the sons of Asaph, and Heman, and of Jeduthun, who should prophesy with harps, with psalteries, and with cymbals" (I Chron. 25:1) The mighty ministry of the intercessors must also rise up with the minstrel to war against the forces of Hell and give entrance for the prophetic ministry to go forth in the earth.

These ministries will accompany the prophetic in order to cultivate a deep love in the heart of the Bride of Christ for the Bridegroom, Jesus. This love will motivate the Bride to step out of her bed chamber, put those combat boots on, and face the issues that confront a lost and dying generation of people.

The spirit of Elijah being imparted to the Church today is drawing the heart of the fathers to the children and the heart of the children to the fathers. This is the ultimate purpose for the prophetic voice of God. It is being proclaimed throughout the world today, calling a people back into fellowship with their Father. This fellowship is God's ultimate plan, purpose and desire. Everything

God does is to secure for Himself a people toward whom He can express His love and kindness.

God is truly refining the Church, bringing it into agreement with Him. "Can two walk together, except they be agreed?" (Amos 3:3) He is maturing a prophetic people, those who will hear His voice and not draw back as the children of Israel did under the ministry of Moses. They refused to hear the Word of the Lord and to become that royal priesthood as God's chosen people called to fill the earth with His glory. They were afraid of God's strength and power. God shook them up so much they asked Moses to speak to God for them (Heb. 12:25-29). The new generation of God's people in this hour will carry a fresh anointing. They will not "refuse Him who speaks from heaven." They will hear His voice, obey His commands and become God's prophetic priesthood.

All God has ever desired is fellowship with His creation. Lucifer, "the anointed cherub," led the hosts of Heaven in praises to the Lord of lords. One can almost imagine God stepping out on the balcony of Heaven and saying, "Lucifer, sound for Me." Lucifer, with his skill and talent, would fill the heavens with God's glory. But one day, God stepped out on the balcony of Heaven and said, " Lucifer, sound for Me"...and there was no sound. The Bible says of that day that iniquity was found in the heart of Lucifer and he fell like lighting from Heaven. God's heart was broken, for fellowship was lost.

God continued to seek fellowship, this time with man through His creation, Adam. Adam walked and talked with God in the cool of the day. He rejoiced in a paradise of plenty until the day that sin entered his heart. God called for Adam to talk with Him one day, saying, "Adam, Adam, where are you?" But God knew Adam was hiding from His presence. Knowing that iniquity had caused him to hide, God's heart was broken once more.

Jesus, the last Adam, was God's only Son. God gave Jesus to us as a gift. He left the glories of Heaven to save a rebellious world. The Father and Jesus were so close that they were one. But God the Father's heart was broken one last time when Jesus became sin for us. For one dark moment fellowship was severed, as a holy God could not look upon sin. God's heart was broken once again.

Because of His chosen suffering and resurrection, God through Jesus Christ opened the door for all men to fellowship with Him. God desires a "holy people and a royal nation" to be His very own possession. As God's people, let us not break God's heart again by refusing to hear the Giver of life, the One who speaks from Heaven. Let us rise up and become God's chosen prophetic people, carriers of the fresh oil from Heaven.

Chapter 10

A People of War—
The Army of God

There is an army of believers being gathered and equipped in these days who will be skilled in all the weapons of spiritual warfare. They will be those who have understanding of the times and insight into the ways of God concerning Kingdom conquest. Their discernment in spiritual things and submission to the leading of the Spirit will give them great advantage over previous generations of warriors both in the Kingdom of light and the kingdom of darkness. They view the Kingdom of God not as a term or an idea to be debated, but as the powerful reign of Jesus, the King of kings and Lord of lords.

To become enlisted in this end-time army one must go through the boot camp of the Holy Spirit and have all the carnal ways of warfare burned out of him. No allegiance to the flesh can be tolerated, or defeat in the heat of battle will be inevitable. God has given the Spirit's power to burn all the fleshly desires out of these "front-liners" and baptize them totally in His fire.

I indeed baptize you with water unto repentance: but he that cometh after me is mightier than I, whose shoes I am not worthy to bear: he shall baptize you with the Holy Ghost, and with fire: whose fan is in his hand, and he will thoroughly purge his floor, and gather his wheat into the garner; but he will burn up the chaff with unquenchable fire.

Matthew 3:11-12

Shadrach, Meshach and Abednego were thrown into the fiery furnace, yet the only thing that burned was the cord that kept them bound. God's fire sets people free. When we are free of self, free of the lusts and carnal desires that weigh us down, then the life of God can freely flow through us. When the baptism of fire burns through us, it will eliminate all the soulish and selfish clutter so that we can be victorious over the fiery darts that come against us.

Forasmuch then as Christ hath suffered for us in the flesh, arm yourselves likewise with the same mind: for he that hath suffered in the flesh hath ceased from sin...

First Peter 4:1

As we allow the Spirit of God to burn all the fleshly chaff out of our lives, it will result in a death process. A funeral for the flesh will take place. Then God will have us right where He wants us. Now He can enlist us into His army of overcomers and we will be armed to defeat the enemy on every score.

How does one sign up for enlistment into this team of "special forces" in the Kingdom? The simple key to finding God is to seek Him. He is not interested in performance or outward shows. When an individual develops a disciplined lifestyle of setting himself apart from the world to seek the Lord, the fire of God will be present both to destroy and to build. The Lord told Joshua to tell the people of God, "Sanctify yourselves, for tomorrow I shall do signs and wonders among you." The word *sanctify* means "to set apart."

A good soldier does not entangle himself with the affairs of this world (II Tim. 2:4). He is one who must sometimes endure hardship (v. 3). A good soldier is under authority and seeks to please the one who made him a soldier. It can be so easy to give in to the will of the flesh or go the way of the world. When we turn to God with all our heart, making a determined effort to seek Him and His wisdom, He will keep us in the hour of testing.

Soldiers who have first committed themselves to peaceful moments of communication with their Captain can fully wield their swords. The Commander-in-Chief will give the instruction, reproof, encouragement and revelation necessary to produce boldness for the battle. Suffering in the flesh means disciplining ourselves to write the Lord's orders on the tablets of our hearts and minds. This need not be a burdensome process, for in seeking the Lord we will find grace sufficient for every need. The army of God is led into battle with peace of heart, knowing the battle has been secured through Jesus' death and resurrection. The strategy for daily victory awaits those who seek His face.

The Enemy's Plan

The enemy's desire is to take something and make it into absolutely nothing. He selects the people with the greatest talents and abilities, convincing them to use those talents for their own glory. He convinces them to waste their lives just making money, knowing it will never make them happy. Being full of hate and jealousy, he takes it out on the Church. He wants us to make the same mistake he did so that we will be pulled down with him.

He is trying to afflict the Church with spiritual AIDS. AIDS attacks the immune system of the body so that the affected person

117

cannot ward off sickness. Spiritual AIDS makes one so weak that he sits back and allows the devil to run right over him.

The "A" in spiritual AIDS is for "accusation." Satan is trying to weaken the Body through the spirit of accusation and condemnation, making us feel unworthy. He is a liar, for there are no unworthy vessels among us, even if we are earthen vessels (II Cor. 4:7). Every person who has been born again has been made beautiful in God's eyes. God has chosen to put His treasures, His precious gifts and callings in these vessels. He isn't looking for golden vessels or silver vessels, but yielded vessels. God knows where we came from, yet He still chose us. Let the enemy be silent.

There is therefore now no condemnation to them which are in Christ Jesus, who walk not after the flesh, but after the Spirit.

Romans 8:1

If God convicts us of some particular sin, that's another story. We receive His conviction, but we reject satan's condemnation. Refusing to live under condemnation, we will not be weakened any longer by satan's lies.

The "I" in spiritual AIDS stands for "intimidation" or fear. Satan has implanted various fears into the Church. The fear of the unknown, the fear of stepping out of the boat, the fear of doing something we've never done before are a few of them. We have all experienced some temptation to fear. God may send us to speak to a person who needs Jesus and we are afraid. Yet Jesus says, "When I have need of you, I will fill your mouth." We must "study to show [ourselves] approved" (II Tim. 2:15). When God has need of us, His army goes by our side. His protection is with us as people are praying for us. His Spirit in us will rise up in boldness and proclaim the Word of the Lord without fear.

The disciples of Jesus were not highly respected people, yet those who listened to them marveled. They recognized that they were unlearned men and decided that they must have been with Jesus. That's what we want people to say about us. God isn't choosing only intellectuals to do His work because sometimes their heads can get in the way of their hearts. He is choosing those whose hearts are perfect toward Him.

The "D" is spiritual AIDS is for "deception." If deception can creep into your life, it will steal the anointing. Satan tries to deceive us into believing that we can have one foot in the world and the other in the Spirit. It doesn't work. There can be no compromise in God. Compromise leads to confusion. If you are confused, it may be because you have left your first love. Having compromised your convictions, you have left the call.

Jesus said to Peter, "Peter, do you love Me? If you do, then feed My sheep. Do you love Me? If you do, then feed My lambs" (see John 21:15-17). When we love God we want to serve Him. That is a natural product of our love. If we have no desire to serve God, we are either under the bondage of legalism or we may not love God very much. Those who want to serve God have a revelation of how much He has forgiven them and how much He loves them. Because they have been forgiven much, and because they have been loved much, they can love God and love His lambs...unconditionally.

The "S" in spiritual AIDS stands for "self-exaltation," or pride. Pride, the Scriptures tell us, "goeth before destruction, and an haughty spirit before a fall" (Prov. 16:18). God is looking for broken vessels. The attitude of humility is a prerequisite for walking in the anointing. God can flow out of us when it doesn't matter if we are recognized and we want Jesus to be glorified. He will desire to confirm the words we speak with signs following.

We desperately need God's presence and the manifestation of His glory in this life. When your husband, wife, children, or relatives have left you and you're all alone, you need the presence of God. After you have lost your job and are lying awake at night, you need the presence of God. When you want to be used of God and no doors seem to be opening, nothing seems to be working, you need the presence of God manifested to you. You can't afford pride. It will cut you off from His presence. Keep pride out...whatever the cost. Keep it out.(1)

Characteristics of God's Army

The army God is raising up today is a mighty army of people with the spirit of Joshua and Caleb. They are bold, faithful and wholly dedicated to the Lord. This army has four very important characteristics.

First, they have godly *aggressiveness*. These warriors know they were created for spiritual warfare and they enjoy it. When the trumpet sounds for war they run to the battle rather than complaining about how hard it is! Because they know their place in the Kingdom realm, they have confidence in the Greater One who overcomes the world through their faith. They also have boldness before the throne of grace and they know how to bring things down from Heaven onto the earth.

Second, they have *godly attitudes*. Remember, your attitude will determine your altitude. Kingdom warriors never say, "It's impossible," "I can't," or "I won't" to the Word of God. They believe they can do all things through Christ who strengthens them. One thing God's army must understand is that He only strengthens us when we are fighting His war, not ours. Many are fighting circumstances and problems that don't have anything to do with what God is doing. Circumstances will do one of two things: They will make us better, or they will make us bitter.

A godly attitude will deliver us from the "I'll do what I want" mentality. Proverbs 10:8 says, "The wise in heart will receive commandments: but a prating [babbling] fool shall fall." Godly attitudes bring maturity in relationships involving forgiveness, humility and compassion.

Third, this army has *godly associations*. God's end-time army knows that they will become like those with whom they spend the most time. Associations will either assist us or assault us. They will either build us up or pull us down. Never associate with the devil's losers. Get involved with people who are going somewhere with God.

Godly association also means being in covenant with a local church that knows its place in God's army and is hearing what the Spirit is saying. Whenever the doors are open these warriors show up for the battle. They take their place in the move of God and are fitly framed in the body, supplying their part.

Fourth, these believers have *godly applications*. True veterans in God's army put themselves in positions where they must obey God's Word. A godly application of God's Word is "obedience." Obedience is the only way to experience the Kingdom. A godly application sees the *opportunity* for victory, not the *obstacle* for defeat. It sees the *potential*, not the *problem*. The more we do what we know, the more we know what to do. God is challenging His army in this hour to implicit obedience.

God is raising up an army like Gideon's. There are tests to pass, but the Church will not be trampled. Rather, it will be triumphant if it continues to inquire of the Lord and obey His order.

Gideon's Army

Gideon was called to lead God's people against the Midianites. He gathered thirty-two thousand men for battle. That seems like a lot of men, but they were as nothing against the enemy who were "as grasshoppers for multitude" and had camels "without number" (Judg. 6:5).

God told Gideon to reduce his numbers. First he was to send home the fearful and afraid. When Gideon made this announcement to his men, twenty-two thousand went home, and he was left with ten thousand.

We need to make the same announcement in the Church. Those who would rather kick up their feet and watch television, those who only want to enjoy life and are afraid to do God's will should understand that they will not receive a position in God's army. God is separating the fearful and the pleasure seekers from the bold and fiery warriors.

The Lord spoke to Gideon a second time, again telling him to reduce his numbers. He was instructed to take his men to the water and to observe how each one drank. Those who remained alert and drank from their hands would remain. Those who dropped their guard in a desire to satisfy their flesh and lapped up the water would have to depart. Only three hundred soldiers remained. This number is symbolic of the price of the costly anointing.

God wants to see who will drink from His hand, not presuming they can do everything on their own. Drinking from the hand (representative of the five-fold ministry) means that we are willing to submit to the word of the prophets, apostles, evangelists, pastors and teachers. God will use those who are submitted to His servants.

Each of Gideon's three hundred was to take a pitcher with a torch inside it in one hand and a trumpet in the other. At his signal they were to blow the trumpets. The trumpet is a type of the prophetic voice of God. We are His voice in the earth and it is time to blow the trumpet, declaring His Word.

Once the trumpets were blown, they were to break the pitchers and expose the fire within. Those pitchers represent the fleshly outer man and soulish, carnal thinking. Breaking the outer man allows the beauty of God's holiness to come forth. In order for His light to shine forth from us, there must be a breaking of the vessel.

> *But we have this treasure in earthen vessels, that the excellency of the power may be of God, and not of us.*
> Second Corinthians 4:7

It was the manifestation of fire revealed in the breaking of the vessel that put fear into the heart of the enemy and sent them into flight. Gideon's three hundred conquered with the fire of the Spirit in their hearts and the Word of the Lord in their mouth.

Requirements for Warfare

Jesus is preparing an army that "no man could number" (Rev. 7:9). His soldiers are suited up in fine "linen, clean and white" (Rev. 19:8). They are clothed with the holiness of God. His soldiers have allowed that purging fire to burn in them and cleanse them. They hate sin, love righteousness and are filled with His compassion. God doesn't want us to be a sick, tired and worn army. He needs an army filled with zeal for His house, fired up and ready to fight.

In Deuteronomy chapter twenty the Lord announces the requirements for warfare. He describes four types of people who were not to enter battle lest they should die. When applied spiritually to the army of the Lord, it can make a tremendous change in a soldier who desires to win the fight of faith.

> *When thou goest out to battle against thine enemies, and seest horses, and chariots, and a people more than thou, be*

not afraid of them: for the Lord thy God is with thee, which brought thee up out of the land of Egypt. And it shall be, when ye are come nigh unto the battle, that the priest shall approach and speak unto the people, and shall say unto them, Hear, O Israel, ye approach this day unto battle against your enemies: let not your hearts faint, fear not, and do not tremble, neither be ye terrified because of them; for the Lord your God is he that goeth with you, to fight for you against your enemies, to save you. And the officers shall speak unto the people, saying, What man is there that hath built a new house, and hath not dedicated it? let him go and return to his house, lest he die in the battle, and another man dedicate it.

Deuteronomy 20:1-5

The first category of soldiers God says will have trouble fighting will be those who have built a new house and "have not dedicated it." In the spirit, we must understand the necessity of dedicating our house (our physical temple) to the Lord. Our thoughts, desires and the motives of our heart must be yielded to the Lord and His divine principles so the devil will not have an open door to steal, kill or destroy God's soldiers. Soulish ideas and thoughts can captivate and entertain, but the individual who has fully yielded to the Lord in his heart and prayer life will find great victory in the day of warfare.

Another area of dedication is to the house of God or the local assembly. Everyone who desires protection in spiritual warfare must be joined in covenant with (submitted to) a local church. Some of the greatest warfare we experience is enduring or putting up with other soldiers in the army of God. Great victory and maturity comes when we stay long enough in a local assembly to work through the differences and establish life-long, permanent, godly relationships. The anointing flows through people, not church buildings and flashy programs.

The Body must come together joint to joint in God's divine order to release the flow of life throughout it. Left alone, the believer will die in battle. One of the greatest revelations the Body can have is of the need of each member for the others.

> *And what man is he that hath planted a vineyard, and hath not yet eaten of it? let him also go and return unto his house, lest he die in the battle, and another man eat of it.*
>
> Deuteronomy 20:6

The second category includes those who do not cultivate the fruit of the Spirit in their lives. Every believer has a vineyard planted in his heart. When we are born again, the love of God is shed abroad in our hearts by the Holy Spirit. All the fruits of the Spirit (love, joy, peace, patience, kindness, goodness, faithfulness, gentleness and self-control) are designed to be developed and eaten by the individual harvesting the fruit. The fruit of the Spirit is not only pleasant to behold, but it is essential as a weapon of war. Perfect love will cast out all fear (I John 4:18). It is not jealous or judgmental, therefore we will stand united as one Body. It will place us far above all principalities, powers and rulers of darkness. Faith will allow us to overcome the world (I John 5:4).

Joy is the strength of our life. A man without self-control is like a city built without walls. Patience will undergird faith when the going is rough! Do we think we can win the war without these fruits actively working in our lives? God exhorted those without fruit to return home lest they die in battle. When God is finished with His army, it's going to be as gentle as a dove, but as wise as a serpent.

> *And what man is there that hath betrothed a wife, and hath not taken her? let him go and return unto his house, lest he die in the battle, and another man take her.*
>
> Deuteronomy 20:7

125

The third category consists of those who haven't kept covenant. In this hour, God is shaking everything that can be shaken. He is shaking us into a strict accounting of our priorities, especially where our covenants are concerned. Central to God's heart are the commitments that we have made throughout our life. The husband-wife relationship is an extremely important covenant to which God exhorts us to give adequate time and attention. Our ministries are only as strong as our covenants of marriage. If the married life is mixed up, the ministry will suffer as well. God will honor a person by allowing him to minister under the anointing of warfare if they honor this priority especially.

Not only is marriage a vital covenant to hold precious, but family relationships are also precious to the Father's heart. Abraham was honored by God, for God knew he would command his children after Him. God is calling for strong spiritual fathers and mothers to give special time to their children, God's new seed. Money, success and the pressures of life should not dictate to us the schedule we keep with our children. Their hearts are crying out for attention, love and instruction, and we are the ones responsible to God for their well-being. Parents, your ministry outside the home will benefit from the covenant priority you keep inside the home.

The believer's covenant with the local assembly will most certainly ward off the devil and keep him strong in battle. The house of God is designed by God as a source of spiritual, soulish and bodily strength. Many charismatics (or "cruisamatics") are hopping from church to church to find the perfect place. Sadly, they are being beaten by the devil in the process. A great challenge confronts a believer when he discovers that the pastor and the church members aren't perfect. Now what does he do? If he stays he must confront the differences and iron out the wrinkles, which involves work. Most people don't want to pay that price. Just like divorce, it is easier to split than to fit.

> *And the officers shall speak further unto the people, and they shall say, What man is there that is fearful and fainthearted? let him go and return unto his house, lest his brethren's heart faint as well as his heart.*
>
> Deuteronomy 20:8

The fourth category of people are those who are fearful and fainthearted. When an individual receives Jesus as Savior and Lord, that person steps out of darkness into the Kingdom of light. Unfortunately, that is where the growth process ceases for many. Churches are filled with baby Christians whose lives are spent focusing on self rather than on the ministry of the Lord Jesus Christ. God is looking for warriors, people who are not afraid to go out into the streets and marketplaces and confront the issues that face the world and the Church. After all, Jesus called us to be salt and light in this world. Isaiah 61 lives on in the hearts and lives of the followers of Christ bold enough to walk it out. As the Body of Christ receives more strength and fearlessness, we will become a formidable influence in society, touching the needy, the broken-hearted, the captive, the prisoner and all who mourn. The enforcement of satan's defeat will be demonstrated through the ambassadors of Christ and His Church.

There will be times when we as individuals must be prepared to stand alone with no one but God understanding the vision He has revealed to us. Most assuredly, God will send reinforcements to keep us from falling and aid us in the heaviest of battles. The love of God will cast out all fear and equip us to kill every giant that stands in the way of God's purposes for us.

If we live for the applause of the world, we will never experience the honor of God. We can trust that God will take care of our needs if we by faith take a step into the world to help another's needs. A fearful man will live on the defensive. A fearless man lives on the offensive, militantly and aggressively confronting the enemy with creative God-given tactics. These ingenious methods, when demonstrated in love, will capture the eye of the world. Be bold, be strong. Our God shall do valiantly. It is He that shall tread down the enemy. When we abide by His requirements for warfare, the battle is the Lord's and the victory is ours!

During their time in the wilderness, the Israelites were led by the presence of God. By day it appeared as a pillar of cloud and by night as a pillar of fire. When the pillar moved, Israel was to break camp and follow the cloud. The cloud of God is moving today and we must move with it.

The cloud was not only for direction, but also for protection and provision. The enemy could not see God's people through the cloud. If they moved with the cloud, they also had all they needed. They had manna to eat, and their shoes and clothes never wore out.

The pillar of fire was for comfort, safety and light. How foolish they would have been to forsake the cloud, for it kept them warm at night. When we grow cold in spirit and lack the warmth of God's fiery presence, when our day is gloomy and everything seems to wear out or go wrong, we need only to ask God to rekindle the fire of His Spirit.

The greatest purpose of the fire of God's Spirit in our lives is still purging us from sin.

> *And Ananias hearing these words fell down, and gave up the ghost: and great fear came on all them that heard these things.*
>
> Acts 5:5

When Ananias and Sapphira lied to God's servant, they were struck dead. The same thing will happen in the Church of the last days because many people who should know better are wallowing in sin. The Lord is telling us to become much more serious about sin.

But those things, which God before had shewed by the mouth of all his prophets, that Christ should suffer, he hath so fulfilled. Repent ye therefore, and be converted, that your sins may be blotted out, when the times of refreshing shall come from the presence of the Lord. And he shall send Jesus Christ, which before was preached unto you: whom the heaven must receive until the times of restitution of all things, which God hath spoken by the mouth of all his holy prophets since the world began.

Acts 3:18-21

God is calling His children to repentance. He is calling us to fall upon our faces and weep between the porch and the altar. He is calling us to rend our hearts before Him, to open our hearts and allow the fire of God to purge us of the chaff and the evil in our lives. God is calling for soberness and a contrite heart. This is not a time to fall back, as many are doing. It is a time to eagerly press in and move forward in the things of God. We are being admonished to "earnestly contend for the faith" (Jude 1:3).

God has promised to manifest His power greatly to those who are pure. As repentance comes, the Lord has promised times of refreshing followed by great restoration.

Repentance is changing our hearts and minds and submitting to the discipline of God. God is calling us to march to a different drum beat than that of the world's order. We have marched in step with worldly ways for too long. Come out, be separate and don't make contracts with the inhabitants of the land. One person's hesitancy and compromise affects the entire Body of Christ. If one part of the Body is diseased, every part of the Body suffers as a result.

God is ready to open the doors and windows of Heaven and pour out upon us blessing beyond what we could ask or think. He is waiting for our repentant spirits. Let this be your day of repentance. Leave your old ways behind to walk in a new and different way from this day forth. God has promised that He will "always cause us to triumph in Christ" (I Cor. 2:14). Let that fire of God's Spirit purge you to the place of total victory over selfish defeat. Become one of God's anointed, radical, front-line, Kingdom warriors!

Part III

God's Provision for the Anointing

For we are his workmanship, created in Christ Jesus unto good works, which God hath before ordained that we should walk in them.

Ephesians 2:10

Chapter 11

The Fathering Spirit

The end-time outpouring of God's Spirit is going to reveal the awesomeness of the presence of God to this earth. In the past God has revealed Himself to the world in the Person of the Son and in the Person of the Holy Spirit. In the days to come He is also going to dramatically reveal Himself as the Father. When the Father is truly known in the administration of His protection and provision, then the world will experience the fulness of God's anointing.

In majesty co-equal, our awesome God (Father, Son and Holy Spirit) will reign over and through the people He has chosen. In order to receive God's provision for the anointing, we must come to understand the Fatherhood of the anointing. The Church is being required to know her God in order to receive the anointing to do exploits. It grieves God's heart when His children have an inaccurate concept of Him.

What is God the Father like? He is a loving heavenly Father whose grace was revealed to all men when He gave us His only Son, Jesus. We can see the nature of God revealed to the world in the Person of Jesus. He is mighty, powerful and all-sufficient. Jesus said, "He that hath seen me hath seen the Father."

Although Jesus is one with the Father, during His earthly ministry He continually gave preeminence to the Father by acknowledging His will as supreme. Jesus said, "If ye loved me, ye would rejoice, because I said, I go unto the Father: for my Father is greater than I." Here lies the spiritual principle that caused Jesus to walk in a state of continual provision. It is the missing link for many believers today. The principle is known as the "Fatherhood Principle." Believers are going to begin to see the majesty and beauty of Father God restored to the Church. They will begin to experience the awesome greatness and radical power that God promises to those who are under His care. Isaiah describes His greatness.

> *He shall feed his flock like a shepherd: he shall gather the lambs with his arm, and carry them in his bosom, and shall gently lead those that are with young. Who hath measured the waters in the hollow of his hand, and meted out heaven with the span, and comprehended the dust of the earth in a measure, and weighed the mountains in scales, and the hills in a balance? Who hath directed the spirit of the Lord, or being his counsellor hath taught him? With whom took he counsel, and who instructed him, and taught him in the path of judgment, and taught him knowledge, and shewed to him the way of understanding? Behold, the nations are as a drop of a bucket, and are counted as the small dust of the balance: behold, he taketh up the isles as a very little thing.*
> Isaiah 40:11-15

Islands are just specks to our great God, yet He watches over every one of us. He carries us in His arms. He feeds us like a shepherd. To Him, the nations are like a "drop of a bucket."

God is so great that we have no one with whom to compare Him. Comparisons are futile. He is the "Fairest of ten thousand," the "Lily of the Valley," the "Bright and Morning Star," the "King of kings," the "Lord of lords." As beautiful as these words are, none of them expresses the greatness of our God. He is beyond words. We have nothing with which to compare Him. He is an awesome God, and we have the privilege of being under His shadow.

> *Have ye not known? have ye not heard? hath it not been told you from the beginning? have ye not understood from the foundations of the earth? It is he that sitteth upon the circle of the earth, and the inhabitants thereof are as* **grasshoppers;** *that stretcheth out the heavens as a curtain, and spreadeth them out as a tent to dwell in: that bringeth the princes to nothing; he maketh the judges of the earth as vanity.*
>
> Isaiah 40:21-23

This is our heritage as God's children. When we understand the provision of God our Father, we feel safe and secure. He is the Source of all life, the Sustainer of all life, the Provider of all things, the Omnipotent One. He is the Strength of our life.

When God's children have a knowledge of the God of the anointing it becomes a natural thing for them to love and submit to Him. Our hearts yearn for this kind of divine authority. The Father yearns to provide His authority for us. "Fear not, little flock; for it is your Father's good pleasure to give you the kingdom."

The psalmist David clearly expressed this in Psalm 91. "He that dwelleth in the secret place of the Most High shall abide under the *shadow* of the Almighty." God has cast His shadow of protection and provision over all the earth. Those who dwell in the secret place shall receive His glory.

When Peter passed by sick people they were healed by the anointing of his shadow as it passed over them. How much more powerful is the shadow of God Almighty that looms over us?

Peter was powerful because he served a mighty God. People followed Peter because he had been with Jesus. They wanted what he had. They desired to receive his touch. They were awed by his presence. This is what God wants to do for us. We are serving this Almighty God of Peter. We are under the shadow of an *awesome* God.

> *I, even I, am he that comforteth you: who art thou, that thou shouldest be afraid of a man that shall die, and of the son of man which shall be made as grass; and forgettest the Lord thy maker, that hath stretched forth the heavens, and laid the foundations of the earth; and hast feared continually every day because of the fury of the oppressor, as if he were ready to destroy? and where is the fury of the oppressor? The captive exile hasteneth that he may be loosed, and that he should not die in the pit, nor that his bread should fail. But I am the Lord thy God, that divided the sea, whose waves roared: The Lord of hosts is his name. And I have put my words in thy mouth, and I have covered thee in the shadow of mine hand, that I may plant the heavens, and lay the foundations of the earth, and say unto Zion, Thou art my people.*
>
> Isaiah 51:12-16

Isaiah mentions those who fear "the fury of the oppressor." The God who stretched forth His hand and created the heavens and the earth, whose hand literally covers this whole earth, is the same God who abides in us and all around us. As we the Church begin to acknowledge the awesomeness of our God, fear of failure and of death will not stop us from inheriting our promised land. Past failures will not debilitate. Confusion and impatience will not cause us to compromise, for our times are in God's hands (Ps. 31:15). We needn't worry about God's timing. We can rest in Him. Perhaps we don't need great faith so much as we need faith in a great God.

In the days to come there will be a holy knowledge and fear of the Lord worked into the family of God. We cannot submit to someone who does not love and protect us. Once the Church sees the Fatherhood of God she will be enabled to submit to the Lord. This will free God to trust His anointing to those who know Him and have submitted to His divine authority. The Fatherhood Principle will be demonstrated to the world as the prophetic and apostolic ministries are restored to the Church. These ministries, along with the other five-fold ministries, will take on a fathering spirit to those being trained for full-time ministry.

God will trust His anointing only to those who have submitted to His divine authority. Without submission to God's authority the Church will not receive the fulness of His provision. In order to have authority, we must be submitted to authority. In order to have the anointing, we must submit to the Anointed and to His delegated authorities in the Church. Jesus, the perfect Pattern, said, "I do nothing of myself; but as my Father hath taught me, I speak these things" (John 8:28).

In this next outpouring of restoration, God is going to raise up many Christ-centered, anointed leaders. These leaders will possess such a fathering spirit that their proteges will possess a double portion of their anointing. Unfortunately, most people would be threatened by followers who excelled them in any way, especially as God has intended for the new army of leaders to excel. God's design is that every generation possess a double portion of the spirit of their father generation. An example is given in Second Kings:

> *And it came to pass, when the Lord would take up Elijah into heaven by a whirlwind, that Elijah went with Elisha from Gilgal. And Elijah said unto Elisha, Tarry here, I pray thee; for the Lord hath sent me to Bethel. And Elisha said unto him, As the Lord liveth, and as thy soul liveth, I will not leave thee. So they went down to Bethel. And the sons of the prophets that were at Bethel came forth to Elisha, and said unto him, Knowest thou that the Lord will take away thy master from thy head to day? And he said, Yea, I know it; hold ye your peace.*
>
> 2 Kings 2:1-3

Elijah the prophet was greatly anointed. His servant, Elisha, was sure that if he stuck with it long enough he would get the prophet's mantle. He was determined that nothing would prevent that and refused to leave his master's side. Elijah tested him, saying, "Elisha, why don't you stay here while I go to Bethel?" Because he loved Elijah and desired the anointing, Elisha's answer was, "I will not leave thee."

Elijah tested him a second time, saying that he must go to Jericho and suggesting that it was not necessary for Elisha to accompany him. His answer was still the same: "I will not leave thee."

A third time Elijah tested his servant. He told him he needed to go to Jordan and suggested he stay back. Nothing could change Elisha's mind. Determined to receive the anointing of God more than anything else in life, he had left his oxen, his plowing and the only life he had known. He would not be turned aside.

When they got to Jordan, an amazing thing happened. Elijah took his mantle, folded it, and struck the water of the river with it. When he did this, the waters began to move here and there until a path was opened in the river—as it had been in the days of

Joshua—and the two of them crossed over together on dry land (vs. 7-8).

When they got to the other side of the river, Elijah asked his servant if he had any last requests. Was there anything special he needed? Was there something on his heart? Elijah wanted to bless him one last time. "Ask what I shall give thee," he said (v. 9).

Elijah gave the young man a blank check. "Ask for anything you want," he was saying. "Just name it, and I'll do it for you." Elisha could have asked for anything.

More than any other thing in life Elisha wanted God's anointing. Everything else seemed insignificant compared to speaking God's word as Elijah had spoken it and delivering the sick and oppressed as Elijah had done. Nothing else mattered than obtaining God's power in his life to do miracles for God's glory.

If he could have anything he wanted, why not ask for a double portion of the anointing? That's exactly what he did. "I pray thee, let a double portion of thy spirit be upon me" (v. 9). Moments later Elijah was taken up in a whirlwind, and his mantle fell upon Elisha. A new ministry began, an anointed ministry, a double portion ministry. Elisha had double the miracles in his ministry, twice as many as Elijah had done.

According to the Fatherhood Principle, God uses discipleship (or mentoring) as a primary tool to reach the final harvest and proclaim the gospel of the Kingdom that has been foretold by the prophets. As with Elijah and Elisha, a leader pours his life into his protege and there occurs a transferring of spirit. This is outlined in Second Timothy 2:1-2: "Thou therefore, my son, be strong in the grace that is in Christ Jesus. And the things that thou hast heard of me among many witnesses, the same commit thou to faithful men, who shall be able to teach others also."

There are definite characteristics that the fathering spirit carries. Those who walk in this spirit are strong role models who know how to patiently instruct new leaders, helping them to set challenging ideals and goals for their lives. They know how to rule their own house according to First Timothy 3:4-5. The mentor shares his life experiences with the trainee and delivers him from common mistakes in early ministry. Even as an earthly father would do, financial assistance is often offered under the guidance of the Holy Spirit. Because of the strong exhorting and encouraging gifts the mentor possesses, in the timing of the Lord, the father will allow the disciple to minister with him, giving him the opportunity and the honor of working with an established ministry.

> One of the most advantageous qualities of the father spirit lies in its unique ability to develop a leader without making a clone. The gifts and callings are unique in every individual and they must be enhanced without being controlled. The mentor knows how to bring the best out in the trainee.(2)

God is seeking faithful men, for Elijahs and Elishas. He wants both leaders and followers. He is searching for men and women to give and to carry the mantle. The Word of the Lord boldly speaks out on this issue.

> *Hear, ye children, the instruction of a father, and attend to know understanding. For I give you good doctrine, forsake ye not my law. For I was my father's son, tender and only beloved in the sight of my mother. He taught me also, and said unto me, Let thine heart retain my words: keep my commandments, and live. Get wisdom, get understanding: forget it not; neither decline from the words of my mouth.*
> Proverbs 4:1-5

In a relay race, the runner with the baton and the one who receives the baton run together for awhile. After the baton is passed, the receiver must run alone. For a season, the one who wishes to walk in the anointing must learn to serve the leader with a heart of commitment and love. Our dreams must die for a season in order for God to resurrect them in His time. The protege puts all his heart into the dreams God has given to his leader. Disloyalty, critical spirits and rebellion in the heart of the trainee will be purged by the Lord. The protege will receive his mentor's mantle of ministry only if he submits to this purging. Those who allow their leader to be instrumental in this refining and purging process will walk, if authorized by God, in an even greater mantle of ministry.

With the rise of the apostolic and prophetic ministries there will be an increase in the mentor's ministry. Discipleship is God's idea! Only because leaders did not govern properly did discipleship become a dirty word. Control and manipulation on the part of leaders must be avoided at all costs. God is not into the "clone" ministry. Fathers, mentors and disciplers are there for guidance and direction. They are not to replace the trainee's relationship and submission to God.

The fathering spirit is on the rise! The Pauls are desiring to train the Timothys. God will have His way in church order and government. The fathers are beginning to say with Paul — "My son, be strong in the grace that is in Christ Jesus." It has been said that "the anointing is caught rather that taught." But the anointing is both caught and taught. Because of the close relationship between the leader and his protege, many things will be caught, but they must also be taught.

The Holy Spirit is the master Teacher who reveals His glorious mysteries to the Church. But He uses people to get His job done.

And the Lord said unto Moses, Gather unto me seventy men of the elders of Israel, whom thou knowest to be the elders of the people, and officers over them; and bring them unto the tabernacle of the congregation, that they may stand there with thee. And I will come down and talk with thee there: and I will take of the spirit which is upon thee, and will put it upon them; and they shall bear the burden of the people with thee, that thou bear it not thyself alone.

And Moses went out, and told the people the words of the Lord, and gathered the seventy men of the elders of the people, and set them round about the tabernacle. And the Lord came down in a cloud, and spake unto him, and took of the spirit that was upon him, and gave it unto the seventy elders: and it came to pass, that, when the spirit rested upon them, they prophesied, and did not cease. But there remained two of the men in the camp, the name of the one was Eldad, and the name of the other Medad: and the spirit rested upon them; and they were of them that were written, but went not out unto the tabernacle: and they prophesied in the camp. And there ran a young man, and told Moses, and said, Eldad and Medad do prophesy in the camp. And Joshua the son of Nun, the servant of Moses, one of his young men, answered and said, My lord Moses, forbid them. And Moses said unto him, Enviest thou for my sake? would God that all the Lord's people were prophets, and that the Lord would put his spirit upon them! And Moses gat him into the camp, he and the elders of Israel.

Numbers 11:16-17,24-30

God will teach us concerning the anointing, but we must also be ready to catch it! God is calling all of us to catch the Spirit that is on our pastors and elders. The precious anointing comes through God's delegated authority in this earth. The only way to receive authority is to be submitted to God's delegated authority and His authority structure in His governing churches. We can drink of the spirit that rests upon our leaders.

Apostles! Prophets! Rise up and govern the people! Trainees! Proteges! Learn to serve! For when you are faithful, you will receive the double portion of the costly anointing!

Chapter 12

God's Ultimate Provision—Grace

But God, who is rich in mercy, for his great love wherewith he loved us, even when we were dead in sins, hath quickened us together with Christ, (by grace ye are saved;) and hath raised us up together, and made us sit together in heavenly places in Christ Jesus; that in the ages to come he might shew the exceeding riches of his grace in his kindness toward us through Christ Jesus. For by grace are ye saved through faith; and that not of yourselves: it is the gift of God: not of works, lest any man should boast. For we are his workmanship, created in Christ Jesus unto good works, which God hath before ordained that we should walk in them.

Ephesians 2:1-10

The most glorious, liberating truth ever given to mankind is a revelation of God's grace through Jesus Christ. The law of God was given by Moses, but grace and truth came to us by the final sacrifice for sin—Jesus, the Anointed One. The law was given as a tutor or instructor, but in and of itself has no power to deliver.

Jesus Christ came to fulfil the law for us so that we through faith might identify with His vicarious sacrifice and walk in the law of the Spirit of life. This may sound very theological, but in common practical language God is saying to each of us, "Child of God, I have made provision for you to walk in the good works I have planned for you. You are My workmanship!" What a powerful enabling ability God has provided for His people! There is nothing more enabling, more edifying, more comforting, more exhorting or more humbling than the grace of God.

> *And God is able to make all grace abound toward you; that ye, always having all sufficiency in all things, may abound to every good work...*
>
> Second Corinthians 9:8

Throughout the Scripture, the number five symbolically represents the grace of God in redemption. When we study the five ingredients blended together that constitute the holy anointing oil, we understand that through grace is God's anointing provided. Man, even regenerate man, has a tendency to rely on human ability, talent and knowledge to accomplish tasks prescribed. A mindset of performing to please God and others in order to gain acceptance then controls life's situations. After a period of time, perhaps years, "burn out" will result. God's way of laboring is through His grace. Through the anointing of the grace gifts of the Spirit, and the *dunamis* power of the revealed Word of God, His work is secured in our lives. This grace is an awesome motivation to conquer any obstacle.

> *"But by the grace of God I am what I am: and his grace which was bestowed upon me was not in vain; but I*

laboured more abundantly than they all: yet not I, but the grace of God which was with me."

First Corinthians 15:10

Since the grace of God does the laboring and God has fore-ordained our good works, then the grace of God is the provision we need to walk in the anointing.

Grace in the Old Testament means "to bend or stoop in kindness to an inferior; to favor, bestow or be merciful to someone." A radical change occurs in the New Testament definition of grace: Not only does it include mercy and favor, but it emphasizes a divine influence upon the heart and its reflection in the life of the believer. Grace becomes a dynamic empowering and forceful ability aiding the life of the believer to be Christlike in any circumstance. Paul tell us in Romans 3:20-22 that no man will be considered just in the eyes of God by the deeds of the law, for the law brings a knowledge of sin. The revelation of Christ in the New Testament reveals the righteousness manifest without the law being justified freely by His grace through the redemption that is in Christ Jesus.

This does not provoke us to throw out the law, for the law serves to bring us to a knowledge of sin. The only problem with the law is that it cannot justify or deliver us from the effects of sin. We are justified (made right with God) freely by His grace through the redemption that is in Christ Jesus (Rom. 3:24). Also, we not only exist peaceably with God through Jesus, but everyone who receives the abundance of grace and the free gift of righteousness shall reign in life as kings and priests (Rom. 5:17)! That means we do more than just barely scrape by every day. We can live victoriously as overcomers. Grace has the power and ability to secure us in Him. After we have fallen, the law immediately convicts us of sin. Grace

147

comes running to the rescue in order to pick us up, dust us off, and keep us in the ball game.

A modern-day prophet received a vision inspired of God in the spring of 1984. Here is his account of that experience.

The Baseball Game

This man of God was caught up in the spirit where he and the Lord stood to observe a baseball game. The Lord's team was playing against the devil's. The Lord's team was at bat, the score was tied zero to zero and it was the bottom of the ninth inning with two outs. Love came up to bat, swung at the first pitch and hit a single, because Love never fails. The next batter up was Faith, who also got a single because Faith works with Love. The next batter was Godly Wisdom. Satan wound up and threw the first pitch, but Godly Wisdom does not swing at satan's pitches—ball one. Three more pitches and Godly Wisdom was on with a walk. The bases are loaded.

The Lord then turned and said He was going to bring up the star player. Up to the plate stepped Grace. No one recognized him and he sure didn't look like he could do much. Satan's team relaxed and he wound up and fired his first pitch, thinking he had this game won. To everyone's surprise, Grace hit the ball harder than anyone had ever seen it hit before. Satan was not worried since his center fielder, the Prince of the Air had let very few ever get by him. He leaped to catch the ball, but it went right through his glove, hitting him in the head and knocking him to the ground. The Lord's team won.

The Lord then asked the man if he knew why Love, Faith and Godly Wisdom could get hits but could not win the game. The Lord explained, "If your love, faith and wisdom had won the game you would think you had done it by yourself. Love, faith and wisdom will get you on base, but only My grace will carry you home."

Now to him that worketh is the reward not reckoned of grace, but of debt. But to him that worketh not, but believeth on him that justifieth the ungodly, his faith is counted for righteousness.

Romans 4:4-5

For by grace are ye saved through faith; and that not of yourselves: it is the gift of God...

Ephesians 2:8

The restoration that God is bringing forth in these last days will be accompanied by a deep revelation of the divine work of the Spirit of Grace. The warfare and the works that are to catapult this new outpouring of the Spirit will be done by leaning wholly upon the might and power of the anointing. Jesus Himself confessed that He did not do or speak anything without first consulting His Father.

In what position does that place a believer who is desirous of the things of God? It is very needful for us to daily press in to the presence of God, seeking His face. God is responsible to give us instruction, guidance and ability when we seek Him with all our heart. There will come seasons of intense warfare for the Body of Christ, but the overcomer will be able to enjoy the fight, for God is the One who will fight through him. This fact bears repeating. God is going to teach us to enjoy warfare—to love beating up on devils in spirit to spirit combat. David said, "Blessed be the Lord my strength, which teacheth my hands to war and my fingers to fight" (Ps. 144:1). We are called to enforce the Lord's victory over satan.

The anointing will flow in our lives because of His provision of grace. His divine influence and unmerited favor on us will lead us to walk in the works He foreordained for us before the foundation of the world. That's exciting! If you are finding it difficult to walk in obedience to the covenants of Almighty God, grab hold of His grace, His ability. Humble yourself. Don't be deceived into thinking you can do anything apart from God. We are what we are by His grace. Our God resists the proud, but gives grace to the humble.

Each of us needs the manifestation of God's grace. Even Paul, the great apostle, had to humble himself in order to receive God's grace. Paul had a thorn in his life. Thorns come with beautiful things, like roses.

With everything beautiful, there is a price to be paid. The anointing is very costly. Beautiful things are always accompanied by challenges. Paul had a beautiful revelation of Jesus. Because of that vision he had a great responsibility to give it out to others.

Everything that is precious, everything that is beautiful, has its price. It costs to have a vision. It costs to have a dream and to be a pioneer. It costs to go against the tide of family, friends and public opinion. Most likely, you will be misunderstood and criticized for going on with God. Because he fears your power, satan will assign demons to follow you and attempt to put you down at every turn. But the good news is this: God's grace is sufficient in every battle. You are not destined to defeat. You are destined to victory.

For though I would desire to glory, I shall not be a fool; for I will say the truth: but now I forbear, lest any man should think of me above that which he seeth me to be, or that he heareth of me. And lest I should be exalted above measure through the abundance of the revelations, there was given to me a thorn in the flesh, the messenger of Satan to buffet me, lest I should be exalted above measure. For this thing I besought the Lord thrice, that it might depart from me. And

he said unto me, My grace is sufficient for thee: for my strength is made perfect in weakness. Most gladly therefore will I rather glory in my infirmities, that the power of Christ may rest upon me. Therefore, I take pleasure in infirmities, in reproaches, in necessities, in persecutions, in distresses for Christ's sake: for when I am weak, then am I strong.
Second Corinthians 12:6-10

The more we do for God and the greater the anointing we carry, the greater will be the effort of the enemy to discourage us. He will buffet us any way he can. He doesn't bother those who are doing nothing. He goes to the churches that are getting things accomplished for God. He goes where people are praying and worshiping God, where darkness is being challenged, where demons are being confronted. Being jealous of the anointing, he will use his corrupted beauty to stop us. Be wise.

Satan hates people who are so full of God that they could be shot at, spit at or cut down with words, and still they would smile and love. Because he is afraid of those people, he goes after them. Satan hates people who are content in whatever state they find themselves. He hated Paul particularly.

We are troubled on every side, yet not distressed; we are perplexed, but not in despair; persecuted, but not forsaken; cast down, but not destroyed...
Second Corinthians 4:8-9

For our light affliction, which is but for a moment, worketh for us a far more exceeding and eternal weight of glory; while we look not at the things which are seen, but at the things which are not seen: for the things which are seen are temporal; but the things which are not seen are eternal.
Second Corinthians 4:17-18

151

God is working in us to bring forth the eternal, the beautiful: love, joy, peace, longsuffering (patience), gentleness, goodness, faith, meekness, temperance—His grace (Gal. 5:22-23). Basking in the grace of God will prepare us for any eventuality.

Many people read this account of Paul and immediately assume Paul had no victory over the thorn. Spiritual eyes and ears can see and hear something else altogether. God never said that the thorn was from Him. He said it was a messenger of satan sent to buffet Paul. With every precious and costly thing from God (a revelation of Jesus Christ and His Kingdom being the most precious), there will be a satanic thorn assigned to keep us shut up, locked up and captive.

These satanic messengers will try to keep us from a place of exaltation or divine promotion in God's Kingdom. Satan's effort to steal the Word and to keep it from widespread proclamation will then have succeeded. The victory that overcomes this buffeting, saving us from defeat, is a revelation of grace through faith. This grace gave Paul the ability to rise up and receive the power of Christ to be victorious over the thorn. The grace of God in Paul's life was always sufficient, never insufficient. If Paul received Christ's power to transform his weakness into God's perfected strength, then we can too!

The divine strategy of God is so beautiful in that even what the enemy designed for our defeat, God has sovereignly planned to turn around for good (Rom. 8:28). God is not the Author of confusion—nor does He tempt any man with evil. His name is Jehoval Nissi, the Lord our Banner. He waves a victory banner over the lives of those surrendered to Him.

God's original intent for man was to walk in special fellowship with Him. God is in the process of restoring us into relationship with Him by teaching us His ways.

Proprietor, which is a business term, means one who works a job because his heart is in the job. He owns the business. He is the one who handles the corporate returns, sweeps the floor and cleans the toilet after everyone has gone. An employee or a wage earner is different. He works for a wage. The Scriptures call him a hireling.

God is after proprietors, ones who will be wise stewards of the mysteries of the Kingdom. He seeks those who will serve Him for nothing but the sheer pleasure of serving Him. It is interesting to note that there are two things that God has designed to produce this stewardship attitude in us. One is called warfare or challenge. The other is called the Word of grace.

There is something about warfare that causes a man or a woman to mature. A challenge or a thorn can do this. For you see, that which we have had to fight for belongs to us in a way that a gift never does. That which we are given and pay no price for means nothing to us.

Salvation is a free gift of God—but what makes salvation valuable to us personally is the death we go through to hold to it in God. "...work out your own salvation with fear and trembling" (Phil. 2:12).

The message of God's grace is not complete until we see it not merely as a free gift, but as an enabling force in our lives. Rockefeller said he never gave anything to anyone where it helped them. God says, "I love you so much I gave you my only Son, but in the end I will see how well you managed and multiplied your resources" (John 3:16, I Cor. 3:13-15, Luke 19:12-26).

Matthew 11:12 tells us that the Kingdom of God is taken by violent men and women. Violent men and women are those who want to do something to make a difference. They have initiative. According to the gospel, we are all businessmen. In the end, we shall all stand before God and give an account of our property and its increase.

153

How does God bring forth these fiery men and women? He sovereignly allows challenges and thorns to come our way and supervises the cultivation of the proprietorship attitude. This cosmic conflict with the powers of evil draws something out of us, bringing us into a place of ownership. Remember, that which we have had to fight for belongs to us in a way that a gift never does.

God has planned for His children to turn every thorn into an opportunity to trust Him. We can use every challenge to increase our faith and stewardship towards God. The supreme goal of God is not for us to go to heaven, but for us to get heaven in us. His character, His faith, His love must be worked out in us, making us joint heirs with Him. Everything beautiful is accompanied by a thorn. Revelation will bring persecution and warfare.

Yet perhaps it is more valuable for us to know that every thorn can produce something beautiful. "...we glory in tribulations also: knowing that tribulation worketh patience; and patience, experience; and experience, hope" (Rom. 5:3-4).

God has cut a covenant with man through the Person of Jesus Christ. God's Word, His covenant of grace, is our final authority and enabling force. God is desirous that we take hold of His faith and touch His grace. We are delivered by grace through faith in God's covenant Word. We know that God is not a man that He should lie. Our faith must be put in His ability—the Word of His grace which is able to build us up and give us an inheritance with all the saints.

None of us can ever be good enough to come to God or to walk in the anointing and bear any fruit. That is why His grace comes to us through His covenant. It is His grace that makes us good, righteous and holy. Trust and believe God, for He believes and trusts you with His grace. If we totally understood the grace of God, we would never again judge or criticize ourselves or others. Walk in the light you have been given. Seek and hunger for more of His covenant of grace. These are the life-changing works that keep your life in the simplicity of Christ.

God the Father is bringing forth a triumphant Church to bring glory to the Son, the Lord Jesus Christ. Out of every church outlined in the Book of Revelation there was a promise given to the overcomer.

To the church of Ephesus: "To him that overcometh will I give to eat of the tree of life, which is in the midst of the paradise of God" (Rev. 2:7).

To the church at Smyrna: "He that overcometh shall not be hurt of the second death" (Rev. 2:11).

To the church at Pergamos: "To him that overcometh will I give to eat of the hidden manna, and will give him a white stone, and in the stone a new name written, which no man knoweth saving he that receiveth it" (Rev. 2:17).

To the church at Thyatira: "And he that overcometh, and keepeth my works unto the end, to him will I give power over the nations: and he shall rule them with a rod of iron...And I will give him the morning star" (Rev. 2:26-28).

To the church at Sardis: "He that overcometh, the same shall be clothed in white raiment; and I will not blot out his name out of the book of life, but I will confess his name before my Father, and before his angels" (Rev. 3:5).

To the church at Philadelphia: "Him that overcometh will I make a pillar in the temple of my God, and he shall go no more out: and I will write upon him the name of my God, and the name of the city of my God, which is new Jerusalem, which cometh down out of heaven from my God: and I will write upon him my new name" (Rev. 3:12).

To the church of Laodicea: "To him that overcometh will I grant to sit with me in my throne, even as I also overcame, and am set down with my Father in his throne" (Rev. 3:21).

Do you get the impression that overcoming is important to God? We have been made overcomers and more than conquerors in this life. Through the blood of Jesus Christ, by His Word and our obedience to love not our lives even unto the death, we can transcend normality and be world overcomers! God's people should be different—special! There is nothing that is more boring than living a lukewarm religious lifestyle without the anointing of God. We are made to live and walk unashamedly in the Spirit of God. That means we can dare to be totally and radically obedient to the Word and His Spirit.

If we are going to be overcomers, then we can't be afraid to be different. We must boldly live and walk beyond the natural and the normal in our work for the Lord. If you're bored with your walk with the Lord, chances are you're not walking as an overcomer. Those who choose to live godly in Christ will not get bored. There are too many battles to fight, decisions to be made and devils to stop!

An overcomer faces many battles and difficulties. Without a fight, there will be no victories. Step out of normality and into real Christianity. The scars are worth it all when we see the glorious victory in Jesus. To him who overcomes God will give a crown of life.

Without the grace of God we would have no victory to celebrate. Today the Church can celebrate the great victory of life over death. Death has lost its ability to sting. The law of the Spirit of life supersedes the law of sin and death. Good overcomes evil. By grace through faith we can walk in the anointing. God freely shares and distributes His gifts to every man, as He wills. We do not have to be smart, good-looking or talented enough to qualify for the anointing. In fact, sometimes it's better if we have nothing to offer Jesus but a willing heart. He'll take care of the rest!

The time has come for the Church to be radical for the Lord. Don't be an average Christian anymore. Let God turn you into another person. Walk in the anointing. Yes, it is costly. Yes, it will require obedience. But by the grace of God you can begin today to live beyond the natural and into the supernatural, where miracles become a way of life.

If you desire this and have never asked Jesus to be Lord of your life, pray this prayer from your heart. Then you can begin to walk in the anointing!

Dear Father,

My life hasn't been what You would like it to be. I stand guilty and separated from You, having gone my own way. I desire to change today and to live in a supernatural relationship with You. Please take me as I am and forgive my past ignorance and rebellion. I ask Jesus to come into my heart and be Lord over my life. I accept His forgiveness and His grace to walk a life pleasing to Him.

In Jesus' Name.

Amen.

You may have already received Jesus as Lord and Savior, yet you know your Christian life has been much less than you and God desire. You have a strong need to live your entire life centered around Jesus. All you want is to walk in His anointing in order to be a blessing to others. If you are tired of being an "almost Christian," then begin a different life today. This prayer might help you to begin anew.

Dear Father,

I ask you to begin to empower me with a fresh anointing from Heaven. I desire to receive everything You have for me in order to more effectively bless others. Begin a deep work in my heart today. Teach me through the blessed Holy Spirit to be sensitive to You on a moment to moment basis. I shall be anointed daily with fresh oil from Heaven, for You have a divine purpose for my life and I shall be obedient to Your heavenly vision.

In Jesus' Name.

Amen.

Endnotes

1. Paulk, Earl. *Spiritual Megatrends*. Atlanta: Kingdom, Publishers, 1988.

2. Jordan, Bernard. *Mentoring—The Missing Link*. Zoe Ministries, 1989.

Additional Materials from the Music and Ministry of Lori Wilke

MUSIC CASSETTE/CD

CASSETTE

Here I Am $10.00

Keep the Flame Burning $10.00

Hand in Hand $10.00

COMPACT DISC

Here I Am $13.00

Hand in Hand $13.00

TEACHING CASSETTES

THE BAPTISM INTO FIRE $20.00

Learn how to live in God's purifying and consuming presence. Being baptized into God's fire will bring repentance, refreshing and restoration.

Titles of this four-tape series

1. Unquenchable Fire
2. In God's Presence
3. Repent and Be Restored
4. Spirit of Elijah

BECOMING GOD'S BELOVED $20.00

God is looking for a people, a people that is sold out to Him with their whole heart. Are you one of these? Find out what it takes in *Becoming God's Beloved.*

Titles of this four-tape series

1. Prepare Your Heart for the 90s
2. What an Awesome God
3. Kingdom Glory in the 90s
4. Well Done, Faithful Servant

PRAYER WARRIORS ARISE! $20.00

...is a call to intercessors everywhere! Arise to an intimate relationship with the Lord. Walk in a face-to-face prayer life with God and know His divine will for yourself and others.

Titles of this four-tape series

1. Oh, God, to See Your Glory
2. Face to Face
3. A Cry in the Land
4. Prophetic Prayer

THE COSTLY ANOINTING $20.00

Miracles, divine authority and favor with God and man are the results of the anointing. Allow the Word of God to soften your wineskin and give you a fresh, costly anointing.

Titles of this four-tape series

1. Fresh Oil From Heaven
2. Sweet-Smelling Sacrifice
3. One Heart—One Way
4. 100-Fold Anointing

FORGIVENESS/DELIVERANCE $10.00

Sickness, mental oppression and unanswered prayer can be a result of unforgiveness. Experience your deliverance through this tape series by learning to forgive.

Titles of this two-tape series

1. Stop the Tormentors
2. Forgiveness Brings Deliverance

THE PSALMIST MINISTRY $10.00

An in-depth teaching for singers, musicians, song writers and worship leaders on the ministry of the psalmist. Learn about this anointing in your life and how to minister in it.

Titles of this two-tape series

1. Psalmist Ministry I
2. Psalmist Ministry II

DEALING WITH REJECTION AND GRIEF $15.00

Hurts and wounds experienced through close relationships or significant losses must be dealt with. In this series Lori brings much needed understanding and healing to the part of us that affects our emotions. This series is a requirement for anyone who desires to endure the pressures of effective ministry and committed relationships.

Titles of this three-tape series

1. Causes and Cures for Grief: Part 1
2. Causes and Cures for Grief: Part 2
3. Healing From Rejection

THE SPIRIT OF A WARRIOR $10.00

As the spiritual warfare intensifies, only those with a militant spirit will survive. Learn the characteristics of a warrior and prepare for the victory!

Titles of this two-tape series

1. Characteristics of a Warrior
2. Prepare for War

SINGLE TAPES

Hidden in God $5.00

Humility $5.00

Ministry of Encouragement $5.00

Put Down the Sword $5.00

BOOKS ON AUDIO CASSETTE

A Tale of Three Kings $12.95

Miracle of the Scarlet Thread $19.95

BIBLE ON AUDIO CASSETTE

NEW TESTAMENT WORSHIP BIBLE
$29.95

Narration of the King James text by Thomas D. Wilke accompanied by a warm background of inspirational music by Randy N. Wright.

TOPICAL SCRIPTURE
SERIES . . . . (each vol.) $12.95

Entire Set of 12 Volumes $99.95

Topical readings from the King James and Amplified translations of the Bible. Arranged to bring understanding of the topic and narrated with an inspirational background of warm contemporary music.

Topics in this series

Vol. 1	Praise and Worship	Vol. 7	Prayer
Vol. 2	Divine Prosperity	Vol. 8	Faith
Vol. 3	God's Kingdom	Vol. 9	God's Love and Grace
Vol. 4	Divine Healing	Vol. 10	Spirit, Soul and Body
Vol. 5	God's Shekinah Glory	Vol. 11	Parables of the Bible
Vol. 6	God's Word	Vol. 12	Spiritual Leadership

A Wounded Spirit
Its Cause and Cure
by Judy Johnson

This book is bringing much needed healing to the Body of Christ. It is not simply a Band-aid on a shallow symptom, but an anointed instrument to bring healing to the deepest part of our being.

For those needing healing of wounded relationships or the courage to trust others again, Pastor Judy Johnson brings the forgiving power of the gospel to a fresh hope.

TPB-128p. Retail $7.99

The Costly Anointing
by Lori Wilke

In this book Wilke boldly reveals God's requirements for being entrusted with an awesome power and authority. She speaks directly from God's heart to your heart concerning the most costly anointing. This word will change your life.

TPB-182p. ISBN 1-56043-051-6
Retail $8.99

Order Form

QTY	ITEM NAME	PRICE	TOTAL
	SUBTOTAL		
	10% Postage & Handling		
	TOTAL		

☐ Please send me the Spirit to Spirit Newsletter.

Name _____

Address _____

City _____ State____ZIP _____

For scheduling meetings or concerts with Lori Wilke contact:

Spirit To Spirit Ministry
8200 W. County Line Rd.
Mequon, WI 53097
414-238-1101